REVELATION RIDDLE:
BLAST OF FIRE

Benjamin Thomas

Contents

Introduction

Contrary to how things *look*, we live in an amazing time. God spoke to the prophet Ezra and told him the age would end in 2,500 years – about 2,500 years ago! According to the prophecy, God refreshes the earth as He ushers in a new age. The seven pillars of cultural influence in society come into alignment with the way God designed them to function. Our children are blessed and our nations are healed.

The parables and sayings of Jesus contain apocalyptic clues. Jesus tells us the current dark times are birth pangs for something new; the last days of evil before we transition to the Kingdom Age of the Saints. The Stone Judgment, the third major judgment of humanity, pulverizes the enemies of the Church and sets up Soldier Saints to lead the world. All those currently on Satan's payroll are judged – humanity set free.

I outlined the big picture in the first book of the Revelation Riddle series, *Kingdom Age of the Saints: End Times for the New World Order.* Over time, governments became infiltrated by satanic forces, who now control them through privately-held central banks and debt slavery. Satan infiltrated Christianity and Judaism with paganism and compromise. I outlined how *the* fourth secular "beast" shown to the prophet Daniel controls the world using three subdued power-centers. The fourth beast, rooted in ancient Rome, exercises power through an alliance of like-minded nations who enact the bidding of the little horn, a satanic overlord. World leaders call today's secular government system the "New World Order." Society woke up to the New World Order after experiencing near-simultaneous lock-downs and the rollout of vaccine protocols after the Covid-19 pandemic. Churches and small businesses shut down while major corporations continued uninterrupted. Meanwhile, the medical establishment quickly rolled out dangerous vaccines and governments forced many to take them or risk losing their jobs. The New World Order no longer operates behind-the-scenes – society began to wake up to the "matrix." Our enemy lost his cover, and now truth begins to wear down his armor.

The sinister forces controlling humanity masterfully executed a plan over the course of hundreds of years to enslave humanity. The fourth beast infiltrated and now exercises dominion over all seven pillars of society: religion, family, education, business, government, media, and arts. Christians fail to rule over even a single pillar! The evangelical church taught Christians to stay home and wait for Jesus to return in the Rapture. As a result, Christians shunned getting involved on school boards and local or national political races. Most Christians today believe the world spirals into more chaos and then Jesus rescues His Church. This doctrine created "rapture paralysis," causing the Church to sit idly by while Satan took over everything. However, we all know God wins.

In my first book I show how God laid out an amazing plan to judge evil and usher in the Kingdom Age of the Saints. He plans to put His Soldier Saints in charge of the earth, geopolitically. While this seems radical, we must not forget we serve an all-powerful God who *never* runs from evil. In the first book, I showed how the religious doctrine of a "rescue rapture," where saints are whisked away to escape evil, is entirely unbiblical, as it fails to consider a judgment *before* the Great Tribulation (a time when an anti-Christ rules the planet). In addition, this flawed doctrine flies in the face of how God operated in the past. When God rescued His people in times of Noah and Egypt, He subsequently put His people in charge. Judgment led to victory, not defeat.

This book represents a continuation of my first book. In *Blast of Fire*, I detail *how* it happens. God uses divine chess moves to put things in place for a *spectacular* show! Nothing can stop what God planned. No man or demon can interrupt God's timeline. God loves to put evil empires down in a single day. Only this time, He plans to complete His work in a single hour!

Most nations on earth will join God's new Kingdom Economy. However, a few will sit it out. Anyone attracted to God's presence experiences glory like never before. We are in for a treat!

After my first book, I received a lot of great feedback. A couple Bible scholars told me that they needed to reread the Bible. End Times teachers almost never discuss the Stone Judgment, the third and most significant judgment in the Bible. Once one sees the Stone Judgment event in the Bible, the puzzle pieces of the biblical timeline fall into place. I believe God kept His timeline a mystery on purpose. He planned to unseal the revelation for the generation that would see it – our generation.

God chose us to be alive in the most blessed days in human history since the Garden of Eden. If you are reading this book, you are called to lead in the next age. It's time to dream again. It's time to boldly move out against tyranny and take the promise land. It's time to discover ourselves in the Bible and fulfill our high calling.

1. It *LOOKS* Like We Die!

*Only fools say in their hearts, "There is no God." They
are corrupt, and their actions are evil; not one of them
does good!*

– Ps. 14:1 NLT

If you follow the mainstream news, our chaotic world teeters
on the edge of complete shutdown. Crime skyrockets nearly
everywhere, especially in Democrat-controlled cities. The
banking system rapidly rolls out central bank digital
currencies and by all appearances soon controls how we
spend money. The Great Reset, the brainchild of Klaus
Schwab at the World Economic Forum, details a master plan
to enslave humanity with specific foundational building-
blocks already laid. Out-of-control illegal immigration roars
down the path to destroy America, paralleling many

European nations. Disease X threatens to eradicate humanity. The Doomsday Clock registers 90 seconds from midnight, marking the closest to global destruction since its construction in 1947.[1] Things *look* very dark.

The doomsday preppers are encouraging people to get ready with food, water, weapons, and fighting skills. The evangelical Christians say, "Don't worry about it, we expected the world to fall apart – Jesus is coming soon to rescue us." The Democrats blame the Republicans. The conservatives blame the communists and George Soros' checkbook. The liberals blame President Trump. Nearly all blame their own government for the chaos, in part.

In the natural, there are lot of reasons to fear. A tiny bit of Fentanyl kills even large animals, and can easily be hidden in food, candy or drinking water. Recently a friend explained to me, expressing himself with wildly flailing arms, that *all* China needs to do is dump Fentanyl in our water supply and "America is done." Admittedly I got spooked when my kids were exposed to kids passing candy around at school since we had already heard stories of neighborhood children dying from Fentanyl in tainted candy. When you have children, you pay more attention.

Many of us either know people personally hurt or read about others injured by the Covid-19 vaccine, often leading to extermination. The "vaccine death count" continues to rise. We observe professional athletes collapsing on the field on live television, with no explanation from the media. Medical

---

[1] Starkey, Sarah. "PRESS RELEASE: Doomsday Clock remains at 90 seconds to midnight." *The Bulletin*. January 23, 2024. https://thebulletin.org/2024/01/press-release-doomsday-clock-remains-at-90-seconds-to-midnight/

personnel simply carry the collapsed athletes off the field and then the game continues – an eerie experience. Perhaps the oddest dynamic relates to parents that lost children to the Covid-19 vaccine only to remain silent. To lose priceless treasure to medical tyranny and then stay mum continues to shock me. Why aren't parents shouting from the rooftops? Does this mean they quickly executed a settlement and non-disclosure agreement? Is the media deliberately censuring the news, meaning parents have nowhere to tell their stories? Given the scale of the issue, it feels like we live in the Twilight Zone.

If you live in the United States, Brazil or many other countries, election integrity remains a forefront issue. Clearly, the election was stolen in 2020 in the United States. The movie *2000 Mules* demonstrated evidence of vote tampering.[2] Voters went to bed on November 3, 2020 with sweet dreams, grateful that Donald J. Trump won the election. The next day, we woke up to the horror after "missing ballots" suddenly reversed the momentum with the media screaming, "Joe Biden Next President!" Patriots called a foul and outrage slowly grew on alternative social media platforms, culminating with a historic demonstration on January 6, 2021. A day of peaceful protests turned into another nightmare after embedded feds instigated violence and manipulated the crowds by opening the doors to the U.S. Capitol, allowing live-recording media plants to film the "violent terrorists." To this day, we can't access all the J-6 footage despite repeated promises by politicians. In a display

---

[2]   D'Souza, Dinesh, director. *2000 Mules*. D'Souza Media & Salem Media, 2022. 1 hr., 19 mins. https://www.imdb.com/title/tt18924506/

of shock and awe, federal authorities stormed patriots' homes in the middle of the night in SWAT gear and locked up ordinary Americans and threw away the key. Scores of political prisoners remain incarcerated – yet the mainstream media reports *not one* corrupt government official serving jail time.

With every visit to the grocery store, humanity realizes that our paper money loses value each day. The daily exchange rates posted on the Forex fail to tell the full story. Comparing movements of the value of the British pound with the U.S. dollar might look relatively stable. However, both the Englishman and the American sense a bag of groceries costs more than it used to – a whole lot more. Society slowly wakes up to the reality that all currencies worldwide are rapidly losing value, as the private-central-banks tasked with limiting inflation fail in their charters – everywhere and all at once.

An extension of the FISA program, which legalizes spying on Americans, sailed through Congress without even a fight, despite proven fraught with abuses on multiple occasions. The most recent FISA extension occurred under the watch of our "new and improved" speaker of the House, Mike Johnson. Meanwhile, when we log on to our computers, we see a "revised privacy policy" from nearly every platform we use. Since most utilize multiple cloud platforms and are distracted trying to earn enough income to survive, we often fail to study the policy details and simply accept new terms. Every time, we know we yield "just a little bit more" of our privacy – a disgusting feeling.

Illegal immigration continues to be an issue for many people across the world. Without public notice or approval, humanity wakes up each morning with an endless stream of new "neighbors" we don't recognize and did not invite into our communities, who likely don't share our values. The "tent cities" popping up in thousands of communities worldwide feature beautiful, expensive and durable tents that consumers would be lucky to find at REI Coop. Worse, in America, our beautiful hotels are filled with illegal aliens who roam the streets, steal scooters, and appear to be living a life of anarchy, all compliments of the U.S. taxpayer. We remember the decades of struggles we endured to create vibrant communities, slowly improving our homes to increase the value of our neighborhood, and working hard to keep our streets clean. Yet a swarm of dangerous interlopers erodes the value of communities in a matter of weeks as crime rises exponentially and basic security falls by the wayside. Our local police forces, deflated by the "defund the police" movement, feel less motivated to protect the communities they serve after being vilified by the media on a continual basis.

What about the global level of debt? Today, worldwide debt approaches nearly half a *quadrillion dollars*, including public and private debt. The human mind cannot begin to comprehend this number. It's a number comparable to grains of sand on a seashore or stars in the sky. The result? Most people filing their tax returns are left with a greasy, ugly feeling inside – knowing their tax dollars are consumed by interest payments, and not used on needed infrastructure.

We feel let down, as if all the institutions pulled a fast-one on us. Now we are relegated to *a* human hamster-wheel leading to nowhere. If we stop paying taxes, our government arrests us, even though they got us in trouble with wild spending. Paying taxes compares with holding your nose while drinking rancid milk. A great number of U.S. citizens simply stopped filing tax returns.

How about artificial intelligence (AI)? We suspect secret government programs paid for the advanced development of AI, evidenced by a growing number of videos online demonstrating robots armed with military grade munitions in "trials" on city streets. Luminaries like Elon Musk warn of the dangers of AI, yet the average world citizen feels powerless to stop it. The latest apocalyptic film, *Leave the World Behind,* paints a picture of complete societal breakdown following a blackout, when citizens are forced into bunkers to survive.[3] Phones don't work, airplanes crash, and wrecked Teslas block the highways. Barack and Michelle Obama are credited as executive producers. What are they trying to tell us? Is this a warning about future planned events? The *Leave the World Behind* plot follows many apocalyptic movies in the last decade that end with no hero, no hope, no solution. These movies are satanic dreams.

What Does God See?

In the natural, everything I mentioned is scary sh*t. It *looks* like Satan is winning. But are looks everything? What do you think God sees in each of these scenarios? For instance, let's

---

[3]   Esmail, Sam, director. *Leave the World Behind.* Netflix, 2023. 1hr., 22 min. https://www.netflix.com/title/81314956

explore the digital banking threat. God sees the lease of the fourth beast nearly up, and attempts to further enslave humanity futile. Desperate elites try to tether humanity to a digital banking system that looks, feels, tastes and sounds like the mark of the beast described in the book of Revelation. However, if it's not the anti-Christ's time, efforts to rollout the beast's mark amount to an expensive but shelved McKinsey proposal.

Consider Klaus Schwab's Great Reset program. Klaus would love to believe *he* is the anti-Christ. As if to project he *is* the anti-Christ, he travels around with a false prophet, much like the real anti-Christ does in Revelation 16:13. Schwab's false prophet is Yuval Noah Harari, a homosexual Jewish author. Harari routinely mocks God and makes veiled threats to humanity, as if he smugly knows the whole program and fooled the peasants. In his book, *Sapiens: A Brief History of Humankind,* Harari says, "History is something that very few people have been doing while everyone else was ploughing fields and carrying water buckets." He then goes on to say in the same book, "Homo sapiens have no natural rights, just as spiders, hyenas and chimpanzees have no natural rights. But don't tell that to our servants, lest they murder us at night."[4] The "us" Harari mentions are the elites, the people who he believes know best – unelected "thinkers" like Harari.

If you *study* the Babylonian Talmud, the primary law of modern Rabbinic Judaism, you know that the elite class of Khazarian Jews don't believe that anyone else has value and

---

[4]   Harari, Noah Yuval, *Sapiens: A Brief History of Humankind.* New York: Harper Collins, 2015.

that certain classes of people, namely Christians, deserve death due to their stupidity for believing in Jesus Christ.[5] In reality Schwab and Harari are *not* atheists. They do believe in their god – Satan. Satan wants freedom from God, because Satan knows his time short and he soon faces judgment. When foolish men like Schwab and Harari gloat in human suffering and mock the Creator, they are simply parroting what Satan would say if he spoke to you face-to-face. God already told us what He thinks about such foolishness:

> The kings of the earth prepare to fight, and their leaders make plans together against the Lord and his appointed one. They say, "Let's break the chains that hold us back and throw off the ropes that tie us down." But the one who sits in heaven laughs; the Lord makes fun of them (Ps. 2:2-6 NCV).

All plans Klaus, Harari, and others coerce are ultimately destroyed by God's plan in a blast of fire. God makes fun of them in heaven and laughs. Does this sound like concern to you?

What we don't see regarding the Fentanyl crisis are the sheer number of people God *already saved* from Fentanyl poisoning. I am certain our enemies are scratching their heads wondering why Fentanyl laced envelopes and food products failed to wipe out thousands of people. A Soldier Saint friend and deep state enemy received an envelope of Fentanyl powder in the mail at home. God warned them in

---

[5] Freedman, Benjamin H. *Facts Are Facts* (Carson City, NV: Bridger House, 1954), 71-72.

advance, but when the envelope arrived, they handled the Fentanyl – it did not hurt them. Jesus promises, "They will be able to handle snakes with safety, and if they drink anything poisonous, it won't hurt them. They will be able to place their hands on the sick, and they will be healed" (Mark 16:18 NLT). Many Christians fail to recognize the authority we *already possess* over our enemies. If Satan could kill us, he would have done it years ago. Between the marvels of the God-designed human immune system and the divine protection afforded in the Word of God, Satan can't touch us. Outbreaks of Fentanyl in a community are most likely because city leaders dedicated that city to Satan and the residents allowed it. Begin to thank God for His protective shield on your life!

How does God look at the FISA program extension and the continuous additional privacy infractions by the deep state? God recognizes Satan's vulnerability. For God knows where all the bodies are buried. He does not need technology to expose the wickedness the fourth beast commits against humanity. Listen to His promise, "Everything that is covered up will be revealed, and all that is secret will be made known to all" (Luke 12:2). Our enemies need technology, including machine learning, AI, search-indexing, etc. to entrap and discover our whereabouts. God needs no such tools – He knows who they are. We are seeing a *flood* of the promise of Luke 12:2 – our enemy no longer concealed. The Internet is not kind to the deep state. All deep state plans are revealed at lightning speed. When they used weapons against citizens in Maui, Hawaii, the truth-seekers came out in full force, exposing discrepancies of the news-media-narrative and even booking flights to Hawaii to expose the truth. The Soldier Saint army is onto the deep state.

Swarms of immigrants cross national borders worldwide, part of a United Nations Agenda 2030 plan to erase national sovereignty. Without borders, all nations ultimately fail. The globalist plan to destroy national identity through porous borders flies in the face of the promise, "He maketh peace at your borders, he puts the best bread on your tables" (Ps. 147:14 KJV). The planned turmoil at national borders allows strangers into our lands who don't respect our laws. Again, God laughs. He knows the time of rule of the fourth beast ends soon.

According to the Institute of International Finance, global debt topped $300 *trillion* in 2023, including public and private debts.[6] I know what constitutes private debt, but what about public debt? As a freshmen in high school, I first learned about public debt from my history teacher. He told the class that countries around the world owe each other money and this is why the "national debts" are so high. I immediately put up my hand and asked my teacher (who happened to be a football coach), "If all the countries of the world owe each other money, then why don't they simply forgive each others' debt?" He stared at me for a long time, but he could not answer the question.

I now know the answer to my question; the central banks that print the currency and set the interest rates in

---

[6]   "Global Debt Monitor: Politics and Climate Finance in a High-Debt World." *IIF*. November 16, 2023. https://www.iif.com/Publications/publications-filter/c/Global%20Debt%20Monitor#:~:text=Global%20Debt%20Monitor%3A%20Debt%20in%20the%20Time%20of%20Geopolitics&text=Total%20global%20debt%20rose%20by,to%20China%20and%20the%20U.S.

nearly all countries of the world are privately held monopolies of money creation. It is to these private institutions the public owes our debt. The world is swimming in debt, and the debt slavery dungeon holds us hostage. In the natural, there is no way to pay it off – just the way *they* want it. So what does God think about this? He's keeping account. In the law of Moses God set forth a year of Jubilee, where all debts are forgiven. The principal legislation and related obligations for the Jubilee include: a) all debts forgiven, b) the release of slaves, and c) repatriation of property to its God appointed owner (see Lev. 25). The Jubilee occurred every fifty years, regardless of prevailing circumstances or king in power. Society failed to experience a Jubilee during the entire reign of the secular fourth *beast*, which according to the Bible lasts 2,150 years.[7] This means we are *43 Jubilees* behind. Listen to David cry out for judgment in Psalm 43:1, "Declare me innocent, O God! Defend me against these ungodly people. Rescue me from these unjust liars" (NLT). Next, we will experience a Jubilee of Jubilees!

Birth Pangs

Are all the horrible things we see happening around the world signs of the end of the world or rather the beginning of something new? If you ask many Christians, we lose all battles in the geopolitical sphere while we live on earth and then are rescued in the Rapture. These Christians expect things to decline until a rescue occurs. They believe the next

---

[7]   Thomas, Benjamin. *Kingdom Age of the Saints: End Times for the New World Order.* (San Antonio: Gloriam Media, 2023). 68.

judgment of our enemies occurs in the battle of Armageddon. However, the rescue rapture theology fails to accommodate a judgment in the Bible which is *before* the Great Tribulation. The prophets Isaiah, Daniel, Ezra and John predict a judgment that brings down the evil cabal ruling our world *prior to* the Great Tribulation. Jesus told us the tumultuous time on earth is a precursor to a hugely important judgment event which leads to a new age. Before the new age begins, Jesus said the world would experience birth pangs. Birth pangs occur before a new life comes into the world.

Jesus' disciples asked Him to answer three different questions about the future, "And as he was sitting upon the mount of Olives the disciples came to him privately, saying, Tell us, when shall these things be, and what is the sign of thy coming and *the* completion of the age?" (Matt. 24:3 Darby). In the next verse, Jesus answers their last question first, concerning the *signs of the completion of the age:*

> Jesus answered, "Be careful that no one fools you. Many will come in my name, saying, 'I am the Christ,' and they will fool many people. You will hear about wars and stories of wars that are coming, but don't be afraid. These things must happen before the end comes. Nations will fight against other nations; kingdoms will fight against other kingdoms. There will be times when there is no food for people to eat, and there will be earthquakes in different places. **These things are like the first pains when something new is about to be born.**

Then people will arrest you, hand you over to be hurt, and kill you. They will hate you because you believe in me. At that time, many will lose their faith, and they will turn against each other and hate each other. Many false prophets will come and cause many people to believe lies. There will be more and more evil in the world, so most people will stop showing their love for each other. But **those people who keep their faith until the end will be saved** (Matt. 24:4-13 NCV, emphasis added).

Jesus points to false religion, wars, earthquakes, extreme famine, etc. as birth pangs. In the last two hundred years, the world suffered harshly. Wars, war-related famine, disease, and abortion claimed the lives of roughly 2 billion people, or 25% of the present day world population.[8] Humanity suffered more deaths from war in the last 200 years than the prior 20 centuries, combined. Earthquakes routinely appear in strange places with increasing frequency. Several false religions launched between the fourth and sixth centuries and more recently. Today, Christian persecution tops the scales of history with 13 Christians martyred (or murdered) *every day.*[9]

Note that Jesus points out that those people who keep their faith until the end will be saved. The Greek word "saved" literally means "to make safe, sound," or to "deliver

---

[8]   Thomas, *Kingdom Age of the Saints,* 72-73.
[9]   "World Watch List 2023." *Open Doors.* Accessed June 6, 2023, www.opendoors.org/en-US/persecution/countries.

from a direct threat," or "to bring safe and sound out of a *difficult* situation." Many will interpret this as the Rapture. But could it mean something else? And what is being birthed after the birth pangs that Jesus discusses? We get additional clues in the book of Romans where birth pangs are again mentioned:

> That's why I don't think there's any comparison between the present hard times and the coming good times. The created world itself can hardly wait for what's coming next. Everything in creation is being more or less held back. God reins it in until both creation and all the creatures are ready and can be released at the same moment into the glorious times ahead. Meanwhile, the joyful anticipation deepens.
>
> All around us we observe a pregnant creation. The difficult times of pain throughout the world are simply birth pangs. But it's not only around us; it's within us. The Spirit of God is arousing us within. We're also feeling the birth pangs. These sterile and barren bodies of ours are yearning for full deliverance. That is why waiting does not diminish us, any more than waiting diminishes a pregnant mother. We are enlarged in the waiting. We, of course, don't see what is enlarging us. But the longer we wait, the larger we become, and the more joyful our expectancy (Rom. 8:24-25 MSG).

Many point to this scripture as a picture of Heaven. But why would the created world rejoice about what happens in Heaven? Other scholars believe the passage refers to the Millennial Reign of Christ, when Jesus rules the world in the flesh for a thousand years. This makes a bit more sense, but what if I told you that Jesus is not coming back until His children move into perfection, and set things right on earth? Plus, the disciples asked Jesus what are the signs for the *completion of the age.* What does this mean? We will get to that in later chapters.

Put Away Your Rapture Mat!

Many Christians are awaiting the Rapture. They patiently check their watch and keep their rapture mats pressed and ready to go, looking to the sky. These same Christians typically don't get involved with school boards, politics, or changing their community. "Why bother?," they ask. If you believe the world declines and then we as the Church get rescued, why would we bother? It would be a waste of time. Many Christians believe in the Rapture, a miraculous event that whisks Christians away out of this world and into Heaven to be with Jesus for a special marriage ceremony, while the earth endures a tyrannical reign under the anti-Christ during a brutal time of tribulation, called the Great Tribulation. The vast majority of Christians believe the Rapture event occurs in a time of great suffering and decline. In fact, I conducted a survey on my *Gab* social media channel that asked a simple question: "When does Jesus come for His Church?" The available answers included: a) The Church is under extreme distress, b) The Church is in a place of great victory, or c) I don't know.[10] *No one* responded that Jesus comes in time of victory – most believed time of distress. You see, the Church is worn out by the powers ruling the world, and we suffer fatigue in much the same way Israel suffered in Egypt. When Moses shared the good news of the promised land, they could not process it (Ex. 6:9). Years of slavery altered their brains – they could only process bad news!

Did you know God laid out a different plan than we were taught in Sunday school? Jesus makes no plans to return to rule the earth until we, the Church, are perfected and all things are made right in the world. It's time to put away our rapture mats and get involved. In 2 Corinthians 13:1, the Bible discusses the concept of God's Word being established in the mouth of two or three witnesses. Let's look at three scriptures that clearly indicate Jesus is not coming back right now. Jesus said, "The Lord said to my Lord, Sit in the place of honor at my right hand until I humble your enemies, making them a footstool under your feet" (Matt. 22:44 NLT). For the avoidance of doubt, Jesus goes on in the next verse to explain this scripture, originally written by King David, refers to Messiah (Jesus) when it says "my Lord." Jesus stays at the Father's side *until* His enemies are a footstool – under the feet of His Body, the Church.

In Acts, Jesus tells us He stays in heaven until a time of victory, "But Jesus must *stay in heaven* until the time comes when *all things will be made right again*. God told about this time long ago when he spoke through his holy prophets"

[10] Thomas, B. (@revelationriddle). *Gab*. https://gab.com/revelationriddle

(Acts 3:21 NCV, emphasis added). The words "right again" in the passage are also translated as "times of restitution," or "restoration." Astronomers use these words to describe the return of the constellations to their original positions. Note the verse refers back to events prophesied by the holy prophets. Could this verse be referring to the prophecy in Daniel chapter 7 when he describes a judgment event followed by a transfer of geopolitical dominion to the saints of God and subsequent fall of God's glory? I believe so – the Bible lists *many* promises related to a victorious age for the Church.

Finally, Paul states, "That he might present it to himself a glorious church, not having spot, or wrinkle, or any such thing; but that it should be holy and without blemish" (Eph. 5:27 KJV). The Church today is not ready to meet Jesus for the Marriage Supper of the Lamb. We are weak, spineless, and powerless. We have allowed Satan to infiltrate our various denominations and there are great hypocrisies within our walls, including pedophilia. Religious institutions, such as the Roman Catholic Church, are riddled with idolatry, *mixing* pagan idol-worship of the sun, Jupiter and Apollo with Christian practices. Other organized churches deny God's power. Many churches today conduct gay marriages, in contravention with God's Word. In the most recent Covid-19 related lock-downs, we saw timidity within the Church in the face of government tyranny. No, the Church is not ready for Jesus to come. Jesus makes no plans to marry a dirty, infiltrated bride that smells bad. He is going to wait for the perfected Church – one that is beautiful, spotless, and shining with His glory. Jesus told us the condition His Church needs to achieve before He marries Her. His plan is perfect and far better than our minds imagine.

When God "Rescues"

In public interviews I regularly call the Rapture teaching of the evangelical church the "rescue rapture." However, "rescue" fails to describe the Rapture teaching accurately. When God rescued in the Bible, He then put His people in charge of the world! From now on, I plan to refer to the Rapture teaching as the "surrender rapture." The idea that God needs to whisk Christians away to save them from Satan's anti-Christ defies every pattern of how God acted in the past. When we consider any doctrine, we need to ask ourselves, "Does this line up with how God operated before?"

With the whole earth full of evil, God planned to start over with Noah and his family. Noah built an ark over 100 years and then it started to rain. The Flood came and Noah, his family, and the animals survived. Who was in charge of the world after this "rescue?" God put Noah in charge!

When God delivered Israel from slavery in Egypt, He transferred all of Egypt's wealth to Israel (Ex. 12:35-36). Then in a few generations, God gave Israel a kingdom. Who was in charge of the world after this "rescue?" God put His people Israel in charge!

Don't Give Up Hope, Church!

God is not planning to "rescue" His Church and hand the world over to Satan. Satan's season to reign over this earth geopolitically *draws* to a close soon. God is not done with America. God is not done with the bloodline of Jacob, the people of Israel (differentiated from the State of Israel). God is not done with this earth. God's plans for humanity are extravagantly *good*. Many in the Church already gave up. The Lord told my mom recently (who is in her 80s) that He was sad that many in her age bracket are tired and ready to go home. They have given up, emotionally. After years of hearing about a surrender rapture, reading books about how God planned to take His children home in the 1980s, 1990s, 2000s, etc., they lost hope. Very prominent ministers came out with date predictions that proved wrong. What's worse, the world continued to get darker and leaders we thought had our back, we later discovered amoral. Scandal-after-scandal hit church groups, institutions and governments. The depths of corruption of the system seem endless and irreparable.

God promises the "wealth of the sinner is laid up for the just" (Prov 13:22). Yet, the last major wealth transfer event occurred thousands of years ago during the time of Pharaoh, when God led Israel out of bondage. Plus, Jesus made no effort during His earthly ministry to topple pagan and corrupt Rome, but rather taught His followers how to take authority over Satan by casting him out, healing the sick, and raising the dead. All Jesus' disciples except one suffered brutal torture and death. No wonder we dream of Heaven – we are tired! The fourth beast, the Rome-rooted system we live under today, wears out the saints. The Bible says "And he [the fourth beast] will speak words against the Most High, and he will wear out the holy ones of the Most High" (Dan.

7:25 NRSV). Just like Pharaoh used Israel's sweat and gifts to become rich, the fourth beast used Christians' sweat and gifts to accumulate great wealth. We are overtaxed everywhere, and the system seems setup for the world to succeed, not saints of God.

Well, I have good news: The reign of the fourth beast soon draws to an end! The end of the tired age we live in today nears – the fourth beast' defeat at hand! The Bible lays out a clear timetable and in later chapters, I reveal precisely where we are on that timetable. We've nearly arrived to the Kingdom Age of the Saints, a wonderful age of victory and revival that happens after a major judgment hits the evil nobles ruling the world today. All creation waits for this moment – even our pets! We live in the most blessed time to be alive, saints!

2. America's Covenant

But the Lord's plans will stand forever; his ideas will last from now on. Happy is the nation whose God is the Lord, the people he chose for his very own.

– Ps. 33:11-12 MSG

God does not forget anything. His promises are unchangeable. He never lies. When God cuts a covenant with man, there is no stronger assurance in the universe that what

God promised to that man (or woman) will come to pass. Satan can't stop it. Do we believe this?

My son and I read the *Rush Revere* book series written by the late great Rush Limbaugh a couple of times.[11] In the series, Rush plays a schoolteacher who works with a magical time-traveling horse that carries Rush and select students back in time to key events in American history, including the *Mayflower* voyage, the signing of the Declaration of Independence, and the American Revolutionary War. Rush explained that he became frustrated when observing the lack of teaching of the rich history of America's formation in public schools, and the ignorance of today's youth concerning the bravery and endurance of America's founding fathers. Nearly without exception our forefathers lived deeply faith-filled lives, with a sober reverence for God Almighty. Rush felt a book series designed for 10-12 year old kids would help, and he wrote a marvelous series. Anytime your 10-year-old wants to reread a book series with words (versus comics), you know the author nailed it! In the book series, Rush does a brilliant job of highlighting how deeply committed our nation's founders remained in their faith toward God and their unshakable belief in freedom and liberty.

Remember that America's founding came at a time just after the Middle Ages, a grim and dark period of world history where religious liberty remained a novel concept. In the Middle Ages, Christians routinely lost their lives for even owning a Bible or daring to stand up to the state-approved

---

[11]   Limbaugh, Rush. 2013-2017. *The Incredible Adventures of Rush Revere and The Brave Pilgrims.* 6 vols. New York: Threshold Editions.

church. Rome merged with Christianity 1,200 years prior and stifled the revival begun just after Jesus' resurrection, as chronicled in the book of Acts. America began with a dream and mission of religious liberty, to practice Christianity without the interference of the government – a revolutionary concept at the time. God took note and protected these brave pioneers, and blessed America ever since.

In the last 110 years, America became subjected to the rule of an evil force against the will of the people through a backroom deal called the Federal Reserve Act of 1913. Since then, America went to war against other nations and kingdoms to enforce the tyranny of the bankers on defeated nations, resulting in great loss of many of the lives of our most precious treasure, our children. Evil three-letter-agencies and bureaucracies formed to spy on other nations and our own people. Now we are waking up to the fact that our government, for the most part, hates us and wants to harm us. We have lost control of our own government. We no longer function as a republic, by and for the people. So is America lost? No. God shows us in the Bible what happens to America – we are restored! As we remind ourselves of the mighty men involved with the founding of America, we recognize the covenant between America and God, built on Bible prophecy, overpowers the enemy's efforts to steal our nation.

The Pilgrims' Voyage

The Pilgrims set out from Southampton, England to sail to America for a simple, but powerful reason – they desired to worship God according to the ways of the Bible, not according to the institutional church. They wanted freedom of religion, without interference from the state. William Brewster, the senior elder and leader of the Plymouth Colony, was fined nearly $6,000 U.S. (in today's dollars) for non-compliance with the Church of England, an Anglican church.[12] John Robinson, the pastor of the "Pilgrim Fathers" before they left on the *Mayflower*, founded a Brownist church, making a covenant with God "to walk in all his ways made known, or to be made known, unto them, according to their best endeavors, whatsoever it should cost them, the Lord assisting them." The group later moved to Leiden, Holland to escape religious persecution but were dismayed at the secular society perverting their children. They sent Robert Cushman and John Carver to England to solicit a land-patent and ultimately secured a land-patent in the New World on June 19, 1619.

Many hardships followed the land-patent award. The English authorities tried to arrest William Brewster for publishing religious pamphlets critical of King James' efforts to impose the Church of England on Scotland. The British pressured the Dutch to extradite Brewster to England, and the Dutch responded by arresting Thomas Brewer, the Christian financier of the Pilgrims. He later was convicted in England and sentenced to a 14-year prison term. The Pilgrims' first boat, the *Speedwell*, leaked badly and proved irreparable. When the Pilgrims finally set sail on September 6, 1620, the stormy season began on the North Atlantic. I

---

[12] Wikipedia. 2024. "Pilgrims (Plymouth Colony)." Wikimedia Foundation. Last modified January 2, 2024. https://en.wikipedia.org/wiki/Pilgrims_(Plymouth_Colony).

suspect the Pilgrims left during non-ideal conditions because members of their clan had arrest warrants from London. The severity of the storms blew them off course from Virginia, and the Pilgrims landed in Cape Cod, Massachusetts on November 11, 1620, just in time for the harsh New England winter.[13] Over 100 people plus the crew made the voyage on a cramped ship a mere 100 feet long and 25 feet wide, less than 2,500 square feet per level – not a luxury cruise by any definition. Many fell ill during the trip. The time between the initial land-patent-grant in June 19, 1619 to the decision to settle the hill in Plymouth on December 19, 1621 spanned exactly 18 months, a fulfillment of Bible prophecy as I will explain later.

That first winter, nearly half of the Pilgrims died. The brutal cold and lack of food and housing claimed many lives. However, if the Pilgrims landed earlier, they would have been massacred, as William Bradford wrote:

> About three years before, a French ship was wrecked at Cape Cod, but the men got ashore and saved their lives and a large part of their provisions. When the Indians heard of it, they surrounded them and never stopped watching and dogging them till they got the advantage and killed all but three or four of them, whom they kept. They sent them from one Sachem to another, making sport of them and using them worse than slaves.[14]

---

[13] Federer, William J. *America's God and Country: Encyclopedia of Quotations.* (Fort Meyers: AmeriSearch, 2017), 63.
[14] Federer, *America's God and Country,* 64.

Before setting foot on dry land, Bradford and the other leaders signed the Mayflower Compact, the first great government and constitutional document in America. This revolutionary covenant influenced all other constitutional documents in America ever since. It starts with:

> In ye name of God, Amen. We whose names are underwritten, the loyall subjects of our dread soveraigne Lord, King James, by ye grace of God, of Great Britaine, France, & Ireland king, defender of ye faith, etc., having undertaken for ye glorie of God, and advancemente of ye Christian faith, and honour of our king & countrie, a voyage to plant ye first colonie in ye Northerne parts of Virginia, doe by these presents solemnly & mutually in ye presence of God, and one of another, covenant & combine our selves together into a civill body politick, for our better ordering & preservation & furtherance of ye ends aforesaid.[15]

The Mayflower Compact represented a covenant struck in the presence of God, expressly for the glory of God and the advancement of the Christian faith. The Mayflower Compact remains a foundational part of American history. God never forgot this covenant!

As soon as the Pilgrims set foot on land, they prayed and gave glory to God. Bradford wrote:

> Being thus arrived in a good harbor, and brought safe to land, they fell upon their knees and blessed

---

[15]   Federer, *America's God and Country*, 435-436.

the God of Heaven who had brought them over the vast and furious ocean, and delivered them from all the perils and miseries thereof, again to set their feet on the firm and stable earth, their proper element... What could now sustain them but ye spirit of God and His grace?[16]

How many countries in the world were founded for the glory of God? Do we honestly think God simply walks away from this covenant and lets Satan have our nation?

The Geneva Bible: Guide for the Pilgrims

The Pilgrims carried with them on the *Mayflower* at least one copy of *The Geneva Bible*, a version translated in 1560.[17] I have a copy of the original Geneva Bible in my study, which is a duplicate of an antique copy held at the Museum of the Bible in Washington D.C. Less than a decade before *The Geneva Bible's* translators began their work, William Tyndale was burned at the stake for daring to render the Old and New Testaments into English. The translators of *The Geneva Bible* remained in exile, driven overseas by the persecutions of Mary Tudor, much like Tyndale suffered at the hands of her father, Henry VIII.[18] I am certain the Pilgrims appreciated the blessing of having the Word of God in their hands on the maiden voyage to the land of freedom.

Little did the Pilgrims know *they* were in the act of fulfilling prophecy outlined in the book of 2 Esdras

[16] Federer, *America's God and Country,* 64.
[17] With an introd. by Lloyd E. Berry. *The Geneva Bible*, a Facsimile of the 1560 Edition. Madison: University of Wisconsin Press, 2020.
[18] Isaacs, Simon Charles Henry Rufus. *Preface to The Geneva Bible.* London, 2020.

(commonly called "4 Ezra"), written in the Bible they held in their hands! Removed from the canon of the evangelical Bible, the book of 2 Esdras still remains in many Roman Catholic and Orthodox Bibles. As we will later discover, 2 Esdras contains *powerful* prophecies concerning the current and next age, many of which I believe relate to America and President Trump.

Christopher Columbus

The Pilgrims knew about America because Christopher Columbus discovered the New World on December 24, 1492, over 100 years prior to the Pilgrims' maiden voyage to America. In my public high school in Texas, the teacher taught students that Columbus went to explore the New World chiefly to find gold for Spain. However, as stated by Columbus himself, the mission related to bringing Christianity to the New World. According to Columbus' personal log, his purpose in seeking the "undiscovered worlds" was to:

> ... bring the Gospel of Jesus Christ to the heathens, and
>
> ... bring the Word of God to unknown coastlands.[19]

As Columbus landed on each island, he had his men erect a large wooden cross as, "a token of Jesus Christ our Lord, and in honor of the Christian faith." When Columbus landed on the first island he discovered, he knelt and prayed:

---

[19] Federer, America's God and Country, 119.

> O Lord, Almighty and everlasting God, by Thy holy
> Word Thou has created the heaven, and the earth,
> and the sea; blessed and glorified be Thy Name,
> and praised be Thy Majesty, which hath designed
> to use us, Thy humble servants, that Thy holy
> Name may be proclaimed in this second part of
> the earth.

Columbus endured attacks by cannibals, mutiny among his men, and great hardship on four different quests to discover lands in the New World and spread the Gospel. In one instance, Carib (cannibal natives) devoured 40 men from the wrecked *Santa Maria*. Despite these setbacks, Columbus continued on his journey to spread the Gospel on several more expeditions.

In a letter penned on February 15, 1493 to King Ferdinand, Queen Isabella and Luis de Sant Angel, Treasurer of Aragon, Columbus wrote:

> To the first island which I found I gave the name
> San Salvador [Holy Savior], in recognition of His
> Heavenly Majesty, who marvelously hath given all
> this; the Indians call it Guanahani...
>
> I forbade that they should be given things so
> worthless as pieces of broken crockery and
> broken glass, and lace points, although when they
> were able to get them, they thought they had the
> best jewel in the world; thus it was learned that a
> sailor for a lace point received gold to the weight
> of two and half castellanos, and others much more

for other things which were worth much less; yea, for new blancas, for them they [the natives] would give all they had... so that it seemed to me wrong and I forbade it, and I gave them a thousand good, pleasing things which I had brought, in order that they might be fond of us, and furthermore might become Christians and be inclined to the love and service of Their Highnesses and of the whole Castilian nation [Spain].[20]

Columbus remained sensitive to trading worthless items for gold, and forbade his men to engage in this practice. These are not the words of a greedy, selfish plunderer but of someone that knew his God and held others in esteem out of a pure heart.

All men of renown, who accomplish great things and achieve the high calling of God discover themselves in the Word of God and move forward with boldness and faith. Have you found yourself in the Bible, yet? Columbus saw himself in the Bible, specifically in the book of Isaiah. In Columbus' book, *Libro de las profecias (Book of Prophecies)*, written around 1501 between his third and fourth expeditions, Columbus cited the following scripture passages:

The LORD reigneth; let the earth rejoice; let the multitude of isles be glad thereof (Ps. 97:2 KJV).

Sing unto the LORD a new song, and his praise from the end of the earth, ye that go down

---

[20]   Federer, *America's God and Country*, 120.

to the sea, and all that is therein; the isles, and the inhabitants thereof (Isa. 42:10).

Listen, O isles, unto me; and hearken, ye people, from far; The LORD hath called me from the womb; from the bowels of my mother hath he made mention of my name (v. 49:1).

My righteousness is near; my salvation is gone forth, and mine arms shall judge the people; the isles shall wait upon me, and on mine arm shall they trust (v. 51:5).

Surely the isles shall wait for me, and the ships of Tarshish first, to bring thy sons from far, their silver and their gold with them, unto the name of the LORD thy God, and to the Holy One of Israel, because he hath glorified thee (v. 60:9).

I am sought of them that asked not for me; I am found of them that sought me not: I said, Behold me, behold me, unto a nation that was not called by my name (v. 65:1).

Go ye therefore, and teach all nations, baptizing them in the name of the Father, and of the Son, and of the Holy Ghost: Teaching them to observe all things whatsoever I have commanded you: and, lo, I am with you alway, even unto the end of the world (Matt. 28:19- 20).[21]

Columbus saw himself fulfilling God's promises in the Word. Being a sailor afforded him time to meditate on God's

---

[21]   Federer, *America's God and Country,* 128.

promises and Columbus felt certain that his own calling involved fulfilling God's prophecies to the "isles." I believe Columbus fulfilled God's prophecies, subsequently paving the way for America's formation.

Washington and the Continental Congress

Several hundred years after Columbus discovered the New World and the Pilgrims settled in Massachusetts, America's colonies thrived and a group of men decided to formalize the freedom experiment by organizing the Continental Congress and declaring independence from Britain. Great pressure fell on the members of the Continental Congress, as threats abounded and the British powers feared the establishment of a free nation. The Declaration of Independence, adopted on July 4, 1776, declared:

> When in the Course of human events, it becomes necessary for one people to dissolve the political banks which have connected them with another, and to assume among the powers of the earth, the separate and equal station to which the Laws of Nature and of Nature's God entitles them...
>
> We hold these truths to be self-evident, that all men are created equal. That they are endowed by their Creator with certain inalienable rights, that among these are life, liberty and the pursuit of happiness...
>
> We, Therefore, the Representative of the United States of America, in General Congress,

Assembled, appealing to the Supreme Judge of the world for the rectitude of our intentions...

And for the support of this Declaration, with a firm reliance on the protection of Divine Providence, we mutually pledge to each other our Lives, our Fortunes, and our sacred Honor.[22]

God is mentioned four times in this excerpt of the Declaration of Independence! After each of the delegates signed, Samuel Adams declared:

We have this day restored the Sovereign to Whom all men ought to be obedient. He reigns in heaven and from the rising to the setting of the sun, let His kingdom come.

The 56 signers of the Declaration of Independence paid dearly for our freedoms. Five were arrested as traitors by Britain, 12 had their homes looted and burned by the same, 17 lost their fortunes, two lost sons in the Continental Army and nine fought and died during the Revolutionary War.

Within a few days of signing the Declaration of Independence, in his first general order to his troops, General George Washington called on "Every officer and man... to live, and act, as becomes a Christian Soldier defending the dearest Rights and Liberties of his country."[23] The following year, the Continental Congress approved the import of 20,000 copies of the Bible from Holland, due to the shortage created by

---

[22]   Federer, *America's God and Country*, 143-144.
[23]   Federer, *America's God and Country*, 146.

disrupted trade with England. The patriots knew where their strength came from.

George Washington, a *devoted* man of prayer, later became president and referred to and gave credit to God several times, and in recorded private prayers expressed his allegiance to God's Son, Jesus. I remain confused why Washington signed into law America's first private-central-bank in 1791, the First Bank of the United States, despite the opposition of Thomas Jefferson.[24] The First Bank of the United States, modeled after the Bank of England, was Alexander Hamilton's idea and served to bring treachery to America. Perhaps Washington did not understand the significance of this bank or was pressured by the City of London, which backed him financially (see Chapter 8). Thankfully, the initial bank charter ended in 1811. Nevertheless, it is evident many of our founders died or lost their sons for our freedom, and they consistently gave glory and honor to God. God's covenant with America still stands.

America Today, the Sword Nation

Since the founding of America, sinister forces attempted to quell America's mission and vision, having roots originating from the Pilgrims on the *Mayflower*. America's mission of "freedom and justice for all, under God" inspired the world for many years. Our founders wisely shunned crowning a royal king and instead adopted a three-branch republic, consisting of the executive, legislative, and judicial branches, each uniquely designed to keep the others in check, and slow

---

[24] Thomas, *Kingdom Age of the Saints,* 58.

down radical and/or disruptive maneuvers. The original design of the founders was a government "by and for the people." Unfortunately, our slow-moving political system proved susceptible to the long-game strategy as well as the deep pockets of the bankers. Using assassination, bribery, subterfuge, late-night votes and other clandestine methods, the elite world controllers – a hidden mafia – now run America. When Congress gave the power to print America's money in 1913 to an unelected Federal Reserve, owned by private interests, America came under the control of the banking families.

In the first book of the Revelation Riddle series, *Kingdom Age of the Saints: End Times for the New World Order* (abbreviated *KAS* going forward), I lay out the case that the world suffers under the rule of the fourth beast described in the book of Daniel. The Bible calls secular governments "beasts" – a great description! God showed Daniel a vision of a vile government system, comprised of ten nations, wreaking great havoc on humanity. In the book of Revelation, John describes the fourth beast as the fourth seal in Revelation chapter 6, stating that "Death and Hell followed with him" (Rev 6:8 KJV). The fourth beast, rooted in ancient Rome, destroys 25% of the inhabitants of the earth. The last 200 years under the fourth beast proved deadly, with genocidal wars, famine and abortion claiming the lives of 25% of humanity.[25] Death and hell *have* followed the fourth beast!

---

[25]   Thomas. *Kingdom Age of the Saints.* 72-73.

The fourth beast is controlled by *a* "little horn" that deceitfully *subdues* three of the ten nations comprising the fourth beast, to affect world control. "Subdue" means "to subjugate, bring under control, to conquer." Daniel 7:8 states: "there came up...another little horn, before whom there were three of the first horns plucked up by the roots." Nations subjected to the little horn literally lose their roots. Oxford Languages defines "root" as "the basic cause, source, or origin of something." In *KAS*, I identify the little horn as the Khazarian Mafia comprised of families of old that control the world banking and finance system (later abbreviated "KM" or "bankers").[26] When America handed the keys of money creation to a foreign power in 1913, we handed them the means to control our economy and lost our roots. Printing massive amounts of money led to bubbles and inflation while reducing the money supply led to recessions and depression. (Remember the Great Depression?) Few presidents or congressmen dared to stand in the way of the bankers controlling our nation. I believe the United States remains one of the three nations subdued by the little horn, as prophesied by Daniel.

Once America yielded to the bankers, we immediately went to war for them. You see, the bankers learned war remains the most lucrative quick-money business on the *plan*et. By initiating wars, lending money to both sides, trading on the volatility created by war, and dividing the spoils at the end of the war, vast fortunes are created by the bankers. The "cherry on top" in most of the wars we fought

---

26   Thomas. *Kingdom Age of the Saints.* 52.

on behalf of the bankers? – they owned the resulting private-central-bank installed in the conquered nation, thus yielding control of that nation going forward. The bankers now had a big, strong warrior (the United States) to go fight their battles for them, putting our children at risk to fight manufactured bankers' wars. I believe all wars are bankers' wars.

Evidence exists that America began yielding its authority to foreign powers earlier than 1913, when Congress approved the Federal Reserve Act. Washington D.C. incorporated as a "city-state" in 1871 by the Forty-First Congress, stipulating that "all part of the territory of the United States including within the limits of the District of Columbia be, and the same is hereby, created into a government by the name of the District of Columbia."[27] A number of treaties were signed with England in the same year. Not including clandestine Central Intelligence Agency operations, U.S. troops fought in no fewer than 45 foreign wars between 1889 and 2023. Figure 1 shows each war involving America and the resulting death count.

---

[27]   An Act to Provide a Government for the District of Columbia, 17 Stat. 62 §42 (1871), https://memory.loc.gov/cgi-bin/ampage?collId=llsl&fileName=016/llsl016.db&recNum=454

Figure 1: Foreign Wars Involving U.S. Troops Since 1889[28]

Year Range	Kingdoms or Nations Attacked
1889 to 1913	Somoa, Cuba, Puerto Rico, Philippines (4X), Guam, China, Nicaragua, German Empire
1914 to 1920	German Empire, Austro-Hungarian Empire, Ottoman Empire, Kingdom of Bulgaria, Haiti, Dominican Republic, Russia, Ukraine, Belarus, South Caucasus, Central Asia, Tuva, Mongolia Mexico (Veracrus port)
1921 to 1945	Empire of Japan, Kingdom of Italy, Kingdom of Hungary, Kingdom of Romania, Kingdom of Bulgaria, Slovak Republic, Independent State of Croatia, Finland, Kingdom of Iraq, Thailand, Manchukuui, Menghang, Nazi Germany
1946 to 1966	Korea, Vietnam, Laos, Indonesia, Lebanon, Cuba, Dominican Republic
1967 to 1986	Korea, Cambodia, Lebanon, Grenada, Libya
1987 to 2007	Iraq, Somalia, Bosnia, Herzegovina, Croatia, Haiti, Afganistan, Yemen, Pakistan, Kenya
2008 to 2023	Libya, Uganda, Niger, Syria, Iraq

Estimated U.S. Wounded or Dead: **1,750,000**
Estimated Non-U.S. Wounded or Dead: **116,000,000**

The over 50 nations or kingdoms attacked in Figure 1 represented independent sovereign empires, kingdoms or republics. The United States with the assistance of other nations, seemed to target nations that operated under a form

28   Wikipedia. 2024. "List of Wars Involving the United States." Wikimedia Foundation. Last modified February 5, 2024.
      https://en.wikipedia.org/wiki/List_of_wars_involving_the_United_States.

of government independent from the "multi-national" alliance. In the case of the Philippines, the United States participated in four separate wars between 1889 and 1913. But why? Could it be that the Philippines has the second largest gold deposits in the world?[29] The narrative that the U.S. fought wars "*over* there so they don't come *over* here" makes less sense when one explores our history. Foreign wars wounded or killed nearly 2 *million* U.S. troops and over 100 *million* non-U.S. citizens.

I recently took a tour of the U.S. Capitol. In the hallways I found a statue of Mars, the Roman god of war, a not-so-subtle admission by Congress the U.S. loves war. The statue topping the U.S. Capitol is the Greco-Roman goddess Persephone, goddess of death.[30] On the U.S. Capitol roof, she appears to be carrying a human pelvis. She carries a huge sword not only on the roof of the U.S. Capitol but in the visitors' center. I believe the U.S. *represents* the sword nation in the Bible, as I will explain later. We are the sword – the military arm – of the fourth beast system, controlled by the little horn. The little horn's religious arm is the Vatican. The little horn's financial arm is Britain. With these three power-centers, the little horn controls the fourth beast system and in fact, the entire world, as prophesied in the Bible.

[29] "Philippine Gold: Treasures of Forgotten Kingdoms." Asia Society. Accessed February 13th, 2024. https://asiasociety.org/new-york/exhibitions/philippine-gold-treasures-forgotten-kingdoms
[30] Thomas, *Kingdom Age of the Saints*, 64.

3. Isaiah 45 President?

*I am the Lord; there is no other God. I have equipped
you for battle, though you don't even know me*
– Isa. 45:5 NLT

When Trump won the election on November 8, 2016, it
shocked Hillary Clinton and the democrats – they did not
expect to lose. In American history the losing candidate
usually makes their concession speech a few hours after
midnight when the outcome is clear. Instead, America was

greeted by a clearly befuddled John Podesta (Hillary's campaign manager), who came out and told the audience "Clinton will not speak tonight." I believe that Clinton and her allies thought they had the election rigged (like Biden in 2020) and were shocked and unprepared when Trump won.

Trump did not run an ordinary campaign. He had no political experience and simply said what he thought in plain language. This refreshed Americans and they loved *him* for it. I remember running into one of Ted Cruz' campaign people months before Trump gained momentum in the election, and letting him know they needed to watch Trump – that he had a good chance. It was clear from his response the Cruz campaign believed there were sufficient character flaws in Trump that made him easily beatable. Boy were they wrong! Ted Cruz got all the free air-time on *Fox News* during the campaign, and then one day, the *s*witch turned off and it was Trump receiving the free *a*ir-time. I believe the networks wanted Hillary to win, and by this time the media had the *Access Hollywood* tape, where Trump told Billy Bush he would "Grab 'em by the p#$$y." News of this tape broke two days before the second 2016 presidential debate between Trump and Hillary Clinton, which occurred on October 9, 2016. Trump apologize*d* but this tape freaked out the Christians, who nearly lost their minds.

The Cyrus Candidate

Just before the *Access Hollywood* tape story broke, Lance Wallnau, an influential Christian evangelist, published an opinion piece entitled: "Why I Believe Trump is the

Prophesied President" in *Charisma News* magazine.[31] In the article, Lance pointed out his earlier meeting with Trump on December 30, 2015 with many other evangelical leaders. Trump told the group they were *soft* and had lost their voice in America. The room did not know what to say, which meant they knew Trump spoke truth. Lance went onto explain how God showed him to read Isaiah 45, a passage about a pagan king Cyrus that God used mightily to redeem Israel from Babylon and, ultimately, rebuild their temple of worship. Quoting from Lance's opinion piece:

> From my perspective, there is a Cyrus anointing on Trump. He is, as my friend Kim Clement said three years ago, "God's trumpet." I predicted his nomination, and I believe he is the chaos candidate set apart to navigate us through the chaos that is coming to America. I think America is due for a shaking regardless of who is in office. I believe the 45th president is meant to be an Isaiah 45 Cyrus.
>
> With him in office, we have an authority in the Spirit to build the house of the Lord and restore the crumbling walls that separate us from cultural collapse. Even then, this national project is likely to be done, as Daniel prophesied, "in times of trouble" (Dan. 9:25).

---

[31] Wallnau, Lance. "Why I Believe Trump is the Prophesied President." *Charisma*, October 5, 2016. https://www.charismanews.com/politics/opinion/60378-why-i-believe-trump-is-the-prophesied-president.

To this day, Lance Wallnau believes his article turned the Christian vote towards Trump. *He* may be right. Reminding Christians that Cyrus in the Bible did not know God but was used by God to restore God's people felt right to most Christians, and they did vote for Trump, despite the *Access Hollywood* tape. One of Wallnau's section headers read, "Soros or Cyrus: Your Choice." When framed in this manner, the choice became clear for most Christians.

On election night, a friend of mine attended Trump's victory celebration event in New York, which occurred in a relatively small venue. (Hillary Clinton rented the much bigger Javitz center). After Trump won the election, my friend casually strolled around the room, speaking with each mainstream media group huddled at the top of the venue. Seeking a response he asked them, "Trump was outspent two-to-one, never held office before, and yet he won. Would you say this is a miracle? Do you think God had something to do with this?" They glared at him but no one answered. My friend had a point – Trump's election victory was miraculous. Our system in America favored the "anointed" leaders, past members of Yale's Skull and Bones society and/or Freemasons. Trump possessed neither of these credentials. He was a scrappy New Yorker who spent time with media personalities and loved the spotlight. He always had an opinion. In fact, Hollywood loved Trump – until he became president.

Trump's Inauguration Speech

Trump's inauguration speech on January 20th, 2017 shocked the world. Usually inauguration speeches resembled vague pep talks with a big "God bless America" at the end. I went back and read the Bushes' speeches. Their speeches lacked any distinction of America from its government. There were promises of what the government could do for Americans, but no admission that our government needed to be reformed. They overused vague terms like "public interest" or "common good." George W. Bush stated in January 20, 2001 that we needed to make our country "more just and generous," whatever that means.[32] His father's inauguration speech delivered on January 20, 1989 contained a peculiar promise, "I am speaking of a new engagement in the lives of others, a new activism, hands-on and involved, that gets the job done." George H.W. Bush Sr. used the word "new" in his speech 15 times, yet later he clarified the "new" he was talking about was the New World Order, which he discussed in his state of the union address in 1991.[33] Trump, on the other hand, came out swinging *against* the establishment. The following is an excerpt from President Trump's speech in 2017:

> Today's ceremony, however, has very special meaning, because today we are not merely transferring power from one administration to another, or from one party to another, but we are

---

[32]   "President George W. Bush's Inaugural Address." *The White House Archives,* January 20, 2001. https://georgewbush-whitehouse.archives.gov/news/inaugural-address.html

[33]   "Inaugural Address of George Bush." *Yale Law School,* January 20. 1989. https://avalon.law.yale.edu/20th_century/bush.asp

transferring power from Washington, D.C., and giving it back to you, the people.

For too long, a small group in our nation's capital has reaped the rewards of government, while the people have borne the cost. Washington flourished, but the people did not share in its wealth. Politicians prospered, but the jobs left and the factories closed. The establishment protected itself, but not the citizens of our country. Their victories have not been your victories. Their triumphs have not been your triumphs, and while they celebrated in our nation's capital, there was little to celebrate for struggling families all across our land. That all changes, starting right here and right now, because this moment is your moment – it belongs to you. It belongs to everyone gathered here today, and everyone watching, all across America. This is your day. This is your celebration, and this, the United States of America, is your country.

What truly matters is not which party controls our government, but whether our government is controlled by the people. January 20th, 2017 will be remembered as the day the people became the rulers of this nation again. The forgotten men and women of our country, will be forgotten no longer. Everyone is listening to you now. You came by the tens of millions to become part of a historic movement, the likes of which the world has never seen before. At the center of this movement is a crucial conviction, that a nation exists to serve its citizens. Americans want great schools for their children, safe neighborhoods for their families, and good jobs for themselves. These are just and reasonable demands of righteous people and a righteous public, but for too many of our citizens a different reality exists. Mothers and children trapped in poverty in our inner cities, rusted out factories, scattered like tombstones across the landscape of our nation, an education system flush with cash, but which leaves our young and beautiful students deprived of all knowledge, and the crime, and the gangs, and the drugs that have stolen too many lives and robbed our country of so much unrealized potential. This American carnage stops right here and stops right now.

We are one nation and their pain is our pain. Their dreams are our dreams and their success will be our success. We share one heart, one home, and one glorious destiny. The oath of office, I take today, is an oath of allegiance to all Americans. For many decades, we've enriched foreign industry at the expense of American industry, subsidized the armies of other countries, while allowing for the very sad depletion of our military. We've defended other nation's borders while refusing to defend our own. And spent trillions and trillions of dollars overseas, while America's infrastructure has fallen into disrepair and decay. We've made other countries rich while the wealth, strength and confidence of our country has dissipated over the horizon. One by one, the factories shuttered and left our shores, with not even a thought about the millions and millions of American workers that were left behind. The wealth of our middle class has been ripped from their homes and then redistributed all across the world.

But that is the past, and now we are looking only to the future. We assembled here today issuing a new decree to be heard in every city, in every foreign capital, and in every hall of power, from this day forward: a new vision will govern our land, from this day forward, it's going to be only America first. America first.

Every decision on trade, on taxes, on immigration, on foreign affairs will be made to benefit American workers and American families. We must protect our borders from the ravages of other countries making our products, stealing our companies and destroying our jobs. Protection will lead to great prosperity and strength. I will fight for you with every breath in my body, and I will never, ever let you down. America will start winning again, winning like never before. We will bring back our jobs. We will bring back our borders. We will bring back our wealth, and we will bring back our dreams. We will build new roads and highways and bridges and airports and tunnels, and railways, all across our wonderful nation. We will get our people off of welfare and back to work, rebuilding our country with American hands and American labor.

We will follow two simple rules: buy American, and hire American. We will seek friendship and goodwill with the nations of the world, but we do so with the understanding that it is the right of all nations to put their own interests first. We do not seek to impose our way of life on anyone, but rather to let it shine as an example. We will shine for everyone to follow. We will reinforce old alliances and form new ones, and unite the civilized world against radical Islamic terrorism, which we will eradicate completely from the face of the Earth.

At the bedrock of our politics will be a total allegiance to the United States of America, and through our loyalty to our country, we will rediscover our loyalty to each other. When you open your heart to patriotism, there is no room for prejudice. The Bible tells us, how good and pleasant it is when God's people live together in unity. We must speak our minds openly, debate our disagreements, but always pursue solidarity. When America is united, America is totally unstoppable. There should be no fear. We are protected, and we will always be protected. We will be protected by the great men and women of our military and law enforcement. And most importantly, we will be protected by God.

Finally, we must think big and dream even bigger. In America, we understand that a nation is only living as long as it is striving. We will no longer accept politicians who are all talk and no action, constantly complaining but never doing anything about it. The time for empty talk is over. Now arrives the hour of action. Do not allow anyone to tell you that it cannot be done. No challenge can match the heart and fight and spirit of America. We will not fail. Our country will thrive and prosper again.

We stand at the birth of a new millennium, ready to unlock the mysteries of space, to free the Earth from the miseries of disease and to harness the industries and technologies of tomorrow. A new national pride will stir our souls, lift our sights and heal our divisions. It's time to remember that old wisdom our soldiers will never forget, that whether we are black, or brown, or white, we all bleed the same red blood of patriots. We all enjoy the same glorious freedoms, and we all salute the same, great American flag. And whether a child is born in the urban sprawl of Detroit or the windswept plains of Nebraska, they look up at the at the same night sky, they fill their heart with the same dreams and they are infused with the breath of life by the same Almighty Creator.

So to all Americans, in every city near and far, small and large, from mountain to mountain, from ocean to ocean, hear these words. You will never be ignored again. Your voice, your hopes, and your dreams will define our American destiny. And your courage and goodness and love, will forever guide us along the way. Together, we will make America strong again. We will make America wealthy again. We will make America proud again We will make America safe again, And yes, together, we will make we will make America great again. Thank you. God bless you. And God bless America.[34]

Trump's speech reflected a passion for what America stood for that could only be topped by a speech delivered by the founding fathers. The speech espoused not a slow steady march toward globalism but an abrupt 180-degree turn back to the roots of our nation, to a style of government whose only purpose it is to serve the people. If you actually watched the speech and focused on the faces of Barack and Michelle Obama, you saw sheer terror and dismay. A new sheriff came to town, truly representing the people's interests.

[34] "Full text: 2017 Donald Trump inauguration speech transcript." *Politico,* January 20, 2017. https://www.politico.com/story/2017/01/full-text-donald-trump-inauguration-speech-transcript-233907

Distilling the most radical statements in Trump's speech into bullet points, Trump declared with confidence:

- We are transferring power from Washington, D.C., and giving it back to you, the people (i.e., lobbyists).
- We are going to stop the pillaging of the United States by foreign interests (i.e., KM interests).
- We are going to stop imposing our will on other nations (i.e., military-industrial-complex).
- America will be great again (e.g., the globalists won't be allowed to steal it).
- A new millennium (1000 year age) is about to be born, unlocking new technologies (i.e., a whole new age will be born).

Trump's speech could best be summed up as a radical prophecy about America's future and the world at large. His speech comprised a sweeping message to the deep state, attacking every pillar of power and signaling their days are numbered. The whole time Trump spoke, listeners sensed he knew something the rest of us did not know – especially regarding Trump's last point about the birth of a new millennium. A speechwriter might include a statement about a new millennium in 1999, but Trump delivered his speech in 2017! Had Trump discovered himself in the Bible?

What Happened (or Didn't Happen)?

Trump winning the election and firing a bazooka into the heart of the deep state with his inaugural speech set off a firestorm. All of the sudden, he went from media darling during his days on *The Apprentice* to media enemy #1. He was accused of colluding with Russia, culminating with the fake "pee-pee dossier" we later found out Hillary Clinton's people created out of thin air. He was the only U.S. president in history to be impeached twice. The first impeachment occurred on December 18, 2019, related to the fake claim he solicited foreign interference in the 2020 presidential election and then refused to comply with subpoenas for documents and testimony. The trial was held on January 16, 2020 and ended with an acquittal on February 5, 2020, despite a strong "Russia, Russia, Russia" push in the media that went on ad nauseam for over two years.[35] President Trump was impeached a second time on January 13, 2021, on claims he allegedly encouraged protesters to commit acts of violence. The trial was held on January 25, 2021 and ended with an acquittal on February 13, 2021, after Trump left office.

Trump survived at least five assassination attempts on his life, including two with a gun.[36] There were likely many more unpublished attempts. At the same time, Trump's own team in large part seemed to want to "assassinate" Trump the "Washington way," by steadfastly refusing to carry out his agenda. For instance, Trump installed Reince Priebus as the head of the PPO office of the White House, the equivalent of an HR department within a corporation. According to insiders, Reince packed the administration with former "Bushies" who simply refused to carry out Trump's agenda.

[35] Dauphinais-Soos, Erin. "Timeline: Impeachment of President Trump." *Homeland Security Digital Library,* December 18, 2019. https://www.hsdl.org/c/tl/impeachment-president-trump/

[36] Kennedy, William. "INSIDE THE ASSASSINATION ATTEMPTS AGAINST DONALD TRUMP." *Grunge,* March 13, 2023. https://www.grunge.com/1224437/inside-the-assassination-attempts-against-donald-trump/

This went on for a few months until "Trump figured it out" and fired Reince, to *be* replaced by John Kelly. Apparently, John Kelly followed in Reince's footsteps and was gone 17 months later. Trump's weakness of being an outsider began to be exposed – he did not know who he could trust.

Despite high turnover and an aggressive media, Trump accomplished more in his first term as president of the United States than any other president in history. Notable accomplishments include:

- Appointed three Supreme Court justices, leading to the overturning of Roe v. Wade
- Nominated and confirmed over 230 Federal judges
- Built over 400 miles of border wall, dropping illegal crossings by 87 percent in those areas
- Achieved an unprecedented economic boom prior to the Covid-19 pandemic
- Passed a historic tax bill
- Eliminated eight outdated regulations for every single new regulation adopted
- Achieved historic trade deals, including pulling out of the Trans Pacific Partnership and retooling the North American Free Trade Agreement with the United States-Mexico-Canada Agreement. He also forced member countries to pay for NATO, not just the United States
- Unleashed America's oil and natural gas potential, establishing the U.S. as a net exporter for the first time in 70 years

- Rebuilt the military, including launching the Space Force
- Defeated ISIS
- Started no new wars (the first president since Eisenhower)
- Retooled the VA and created many other benefits for veterans
- Signed into law landmark criminal justice reform, and
- Cut funding for abortion[37]

The list of Trump's accomplishments could extend further. However, we did not hear much about them. The media remained deathly silent on the stream of Trump's big, bold accomplishments. We nearly exclusively heard about Trump's accomplishments from the man him*self* in campaign speeches during the 2020 election. The media's parroting of the Russia story or discussing turnover in the administration or some other negative story clouded all the good news. Yet somehow America *felt* the positive change. We sensed and believed when Trump made a campaign promise, he actually intended to (and did) pull it off.

One of President Trumps biggest achievements included prison reform with the First Step Act, radically shortening federal prison sentences and curbing inhumane practices in prisons. *The* initiative came about the exact opposite way Washington usually works. Kim Kardashian West and her husband Kanye (since divorced) met with President Trump and asked for the freedom of Alice Johnson, who was serving a life sentence without parole in a federal

---

[37] "Trump Administration Accomplishments." *White House Archives,* January 2021. https://trumpwhitehouse.archives.gov/trump-administration-accomplishments/

prison for a nonviolent crime. Trump later pardoned Johnson and worked with Ivanka, Grassley and others to get the bill passed.[38] Trump did not win any votes from this bill – prisoners can't vote! It really came down to right and wrong. The First Step Act represented the *first* prison reform bill in a long time within the United States, which has the highest level of incarcerations of any nation on earth.[39]

Months before the 2020 Election, President Trump began to warn Americans about how the Democrats were going to cheat in the upcoming election. The Covid-19 pandemic paved the way for radical new voting procedures (mail-in ballots) to open up the door for *massive* fraud. While Trump dogged the campaign trail making speeches everywhere and attracting 50,000 to 80,000 people at campaign rallies, Biden could barely get 1,000 people in a room. I remember meeting a former Secret Service officer in 2020 and asking him whether *he* thought Trump would win. Without hesitating, he said "Absolutely, I have served under five presidents and watched many elections. Anyone who gets these crowds wins." Incidentally, the *same* Secret Service officer told me that President Trump was the *first* U.S. president he voted for in 30 years. I guess this gentleman saw too much during his time in the Secret Service!

So, with all of President Trump's accomplishments as president and the huge crowds at his campaign rallies, why

[38] Bennett, Brian. "How Unlikely Allies Got Prison Reform Done—With an Assist From Kim Kardashian West." *Time,* December 21, 2018. https://time.com/5486560/prison-reform-jared-kushner-kim-kardashian-west/.

[39] "Countries with the largest number of prisoners per 100,000 of the national population, as of January 2024." *Statista,* January 8, 2024. https://www.statista.com/statistics/262962/countries-with-the-most-prisoners-per-100-000-inhabitants/#:~:text=The%20United%20States%20is%20home,nations%20had%20far%20fewer%20prisoners.

didn't Trump "win?" If President Trump represented King Cyrus, as Lance Wallnau prophesied, why didn't Trump complete his mission, as King Cyrus did against Babylon. What happened?

BLAST OF FIRE

4. Prophets and Kings

For the Lord God does nothing without revealing his secret to his servants the prophets.

– Amos 3:7 ESV

In 2007, *nearly a decade* before President Trump took office, a Christian prophet by the name of Kim Clement released a number of prophecies regarding the future of the United States. I saw Kim Clement in a New Year's Eve service in California many years ago and sensed a unique and tangible anointing on Kim's ministry. Kim, also a musician, would play the keyboard and then come out with wild yet detailed prophecies about world events. People that track prophecies readily admit that many, if not most of Kim's prophecies already happened. Millions watched Kim's prophecies online, noting the uncanny and peculiar specificity to which they described an upcoming new type of president of the United

States that seemed to fit President Trump. For instance, in a service in Redding, California in 2007, he prophesied that:

> Trump shall be a Trumpet.
>
> There will be a praying president, not a religious one. For I will fool the people, says the Lord. I will fool the people. Yes, I will. God says. The One that is chosen shall go in and they shall say, 'He has hot blood.' For the Spirit of God says, yes, he may have hot blood, but he will bring the walls of protection on this country in a greater way and the economy of this country shall change rapidly, says the Lord of hosts.
>
> Listen to the Word of the Lord, God says, I will put at your helm for two terms a president that will pray, but he will not be a praying president when he starts.[40]

The prophecy, declaring "Trump shall be a Trumpet" seemed a direct message that God raised up President Trump as His man. People also paid attention to the word about "hot blood." Trump always fired back at critics and never apologized. He eviscerated his opponents verbally and made up catchy names for them that seemed to stick. (Remember "Crooked Hillary" and "Lying Ted?") Hot blood? Check. Kim also mentioned God's president would be a praying president, although not at first. Despite Trump's tough shell, people close to Trump saw him display great reverence for

---

[40] Strang, Steve. "2007 Kim Clement Prophecy: 'I Will Put at Your Helm for Two Terms a President That Will Pray'." *Charisma,* August 21, 2020. https://mycharisma.com/blogs/the-strang-report/2007-kim-clement-prophecy-i-will-put-at-your-helm-for-two-terms-a-president-that-will-pray/

the things of God and always allow others to pray over him. A friend of mine in a handshake lineup for Trump told President Trump he was praying for him. President Trump, now three people down, stopped and came back to my friend and personally thanked him for his prayers.

I believe Trump began his presidency as a "baby Christian" and along the way learned to hear God's voice. Seven years after Kim's first prophecy, on February 22, 2014, more than a *year* before Trump announced he would run, Clement prophesied again:

> And the Spirit of God said, "This man will throttle the enemies of Israel. This man will throttle the enemies of the West. And there are highly embarrassing moments that are about to occur for many, many politicians in this nation. There will be a shaking amongst, there will be a shaking amongst the Democrats in the upcoming elections, but unsettling for the Republicans." Why is God doing this? For God said, "I am dissatisfied with what emerges from both parties."
>
> And then there is a nation *He* showed me, He took me, itching for a new kind of war with America. They will shout, "Impeach, impeach," they say. But nay. This nation shall come very suddenly, but it shall not come in the time of President Obama. It shall come when this new one arises. My David, that I have set aside for this nation ... They will shout, "Impeach, impeach!" but this will not happen.

God says, "Once you recognize the man that I have raised up, pray. For the enemy will do everything in its power to put a witch in the White House." For Jezebel has chased away the prophets and even Elijah. Now I have said, "Go back." For this shall be dismantled so that there will be no more corruption in the White House, says the Spirit.

Here a few things are revealed that in hindsight seem quite clear. One is that the man in the prophecy will shake up Washington and be hated by both parties as a disruptive force. Second, this man would be impeached twice. Not only did Kim mention the word "impeach" twice in a phrase, but he also mentioned the phrase "impeach, impeach" two times. President Trump is the only president in U.S. history to be impeached twice! That God considers this man to be His "David," I will delve into more later.

It's fascinating that Kim proclaims a nation comes against America. Which nation could God be speaking about? I believe this speaks to the foreign interference in our election. We eventually find out that dark forces and foreign interests pulled out all the stops to prevent President Trump from serving again, if ever. When God speaks of nations in the Bible, He refers to secular and organized people groups. In this case, I believe God refers to the little horn, the unseen mafia ruling our nation. President Trump represents an existential threat to them.

The final observation on Kim's prophecy and the "gotcha" for many people says that the man we can safely assume by all the other references in the prophecy is President Trump, will serve *two terms*. Did Kim Clement "miss God" in this prophecy? Maybe, but perhaps there is more to the story. Kim carries a legacy of credibility in the prophetic world. He clearly saw things many years in the future that few others saw. In the previous chapter I discussed how Lance Wallnau also prophesied that Trump represented a modern King Cyrus candidate. King Cyrus of the Bible completed his objective and destroyed Babylon, yet it *appears* President Trump failed his mission. Does this mean that both Kim and Lance got it wrong or worse, are "false prophets?" Would it surprise you if I told you they heard God and *we* missed it?

Two Presidents

On March 4, 2008, *eight years* before the 2016 election, Kim Clement released another radical prophecy describing a time in America of two presidents. In the prophecy, Clement says:

> And they shall say, "But now there is a second president, how can we have two presidents?" An unusual thing isn't it? says the Spirit of the Lord. Why would it be that one with a double *mind* would stand up and face the people? No they shall say, "We have two presidents, but what shall we do now?" Fear not, for God said, as I promised before, this is my nation, and I will change things according to the time and season. And I told you,

now I will expose and reveal things that have been hidden, so that my nation can move into this next election and to the next phase with victory and honor and glory, says the Lord of hosts.

What was Clement saying? How *could* there be two presidents in America? In the prophecy, he also talks about exposure at the hand of God, so *that* "my nation can move into this next election ... with victory and honor and glory." I discuss what I believe this means in Chapter 6.

God's Prophets

God taught me early in my faith walk that judging men and women of God, especially pastors and prophets, can be dangerous. For instance, many years ago an evangelist named Jimmy Swaggart fell hard after he publicly judged Marvin Gorman, essentially for the same sin he himself committed. Swaggart struggled with sin for many years, and I know God sent many ministers with words of knowledge to Jimmy to warn him to get free for years prior to his fall.[41] You see, God is merciful and wants to help His children get free from the grips of sin – and He will help us through it. The Bible states, "It is the glory of God to conceal a thing: But the honour of kings is to search out a matter" (Prov 25:2 KJV). When we publicly attack God's messengers, we put ourselves in danger of losing our own protective covering. Listen to this warning:

---

[41]   "The day after Marvin Gorman confronted Jimmy Swaggart with...." *UPI*, February 27, 1988. https://www.upi.com/Archives/1988/02/27/The-day-after-Marvin-Gorman-confronted-Jimmy-Swaggart-with/7253572936400/

The LORD, the God of their ancestors, repeatedly sent his prophets to warn them, for he had compassion on his people and his Temple. But the people mocked these messengers of God and despised their words. They scoffed at the prophets until the LORD's anger could no longer be restrained and nothing could be done (2 Chron. 36:15-16 NLT).

In this passage, God wanted to save Israel and sent His messengers to warn them, but because they mocked the prophets, God allowed them to be judged. Do you know that by mocking the prophets God sent Israel lost their kingdom and ushered in the rule of Babylon? The Babylonian rule launched the times of the Gentiles that we still suffer under today. We are commanded to "Never *restrain* or put out the fire of the Holy Spirit. And don't be one who scorns prophecies, but be faithful to examine them by putting them to the test, and afterward hold tightly to what has proven to be right. Avoid every appearance of evil" (1 Thess. 5:19-22 TPT).

Before the 2020 election, many prophets came to the table with prophetic words about President Trump's second term and that he would win the election. After January 20, 2021, a significant effort went forth by certain members of the Body of Christ to silence, humiliate and scorn these same prophets, calling them "false prophets." Specifically, a demand began to circulate to prophets to "publicly apologize" for their errors. The media piled onto this effort and began shaming prophets publicly. While I was surprised that things did not appear to turn out the way that we wanted in 2020, I decided to instead go into prayer and ask God what He was doing. In reality, I *knew* Trump won the election – later stolen. At the same time, I was *confused* at what I saw in the natural. Rather than judge the prophets, I decided to ask God how *I may have misunderstood.* Over the course of the next two years God miraculously opened up the Bible to me in unexpected ways. Had I joined the crowd and been quick to judge the prophets, God may have chosen someone else to unseal the books of Daniel, Revelation, and now 2 Esdras. Church, be careful not to judge God's prophets. Remember how many times Jesus said things His followers did not understand, but they hung on because they knew He knew more than they did. Many of the world's most renowned prophets in the Bible prophesied things in their lifetimes that are *still yet to occur.* Does this make them false prophets?

A word of advice; when you don't understand what a prophet says, stay silent. In the remainder of this book, you will find out that Kim Clement, Lance Wallnau, and all the other prophets heard from God correctly. How Trump fulfilled these prophecies and what happens next based on additional prophecies from the Bible is *wild.*

King Cyrus and Modern Parallels to Trump

In the Bible, King Cyrus served as the first king of Persia after defeating Babylon. He funded Israel's reconstruction of the Temple, which the Babylonians previously destroyed.

Every Old Testament prophet whose work became biblical canon acknowledged the role of King Cyrus. Said another way, prophets that disqualified the role of King Cyrus did not make it into our Bible. King Cyrus, in simple terms, worshiped idols. Yet God used King Cyrus to deliver His people Israel. King Cyrus possessed a heart of righteousness despite his idolatry. Listen to King Cyrus' proclamation:

> From Cyrus King of Persia, a Proclamation: GOD, the God of the heavens, has given me all the kingdoms of the earth. He has also assigned me to build him a Temple of worship in Jerusalem, Judah. Who among you belongs to his people? God be with you! Go to Jerusalem which is in Judah and build The Temple of GOD, the God of Israel, Jerusalem's God. Those who stay behind, wherever they happen to live, will support them with silver, gold, tools, and pack animals, along with Freewill-Offerings for The Temple of God in Jerusalem (Ezra 1:2-4 MSG).

The passage indicates Cyrus heard from God. He acknowledged that God gave him all earth's kingdoms. He knew God gave him an assignment to make a way for the Judean Temple to be rebuilt and pledged his support. The prophet Isaiah refers to King Cyrus as God's anointed, representing the only foreigner in the Bible to be identified as such. Isaiah said of Cyrus:

> The LORD has chosen Cyrus to be king! He has appointed him to conquer nations; he sends him

to strip kings of their power; the LORD will open the gates of cities for him. To Cyrus the LORD says, "I myself will prepare your way, levelling mountains and hills. I will break down bronze gates and smash their iron bars. I will give you treasures from dark, secret places; then you will know that I am the LORD, and that the God of Israel has called you by name. I appoint you to help my servant Israel, the people that I have chosen. I have given you great honour, although you do not know me (Isa. 45:1-4 GNB).

From scripture, we learn God called a man who did not know Him to fight God's battle against corrupt kings and save His children. Here we learn that Cyrus levels mountains and hills, which in the Bible represent governments. He breaks down safeguards and defenses. He plunders treasure hidden away in secret places. He also strips evil kings of their power.

God raised up King Cyrus for a special purpose – to redeem His people from bondage. The way that Cyrus overthrew Babylon is a pattern for the way God overthrows modern-day Babylon in the book of Revelation. Just as Herod plotted to kill Jesus at birth, there was a plot to kill Cyrus as soon as he was born. Cyrus' grandfather Astyages, ruled ancient Media from 585-550 BC.[42] While Cyrus' mother Mandane was Median, his father Cambyses was Persian. Astyages began having dreams about his daughter Mandane

---

[42] Jones, Stephen E. "How Cyrus Conquered Babylon." *GodsKingdom,* June 2015, Issue #323. https://godskingdom.org/studies/ffi-newsletter/2015/how-cyrus-conquered-babylon/

bearing a great conquerer-son. Upon the birth of his grandson Cyrus, he arranged for him to be killed. But through a divine switch, God foiled the plot. Cyrus grew up a herdsman, a fulfillment of Isaiah 44:28, foreshadowing the Messiah Jesus, called "the great Shepherd of the sheep" in Hebrews 13:20 (NLT).

When King Astyages discovered Harpagus failed to carry out the directive to kill Cyrus, he killed Harpagus' son and deceptively fed Harpagus his own son at a feast. Harpagus never forgot this, and later coordinated with the Median nobles to support the rise of Cyrus against Astyages, leading to the Medes coming under Persian rule under King Cyrus. Ultimately, the rage of crimes against children led to the rise of King Cyrus, a foreshadow of today's unified battle against the fourth beast, who encourages abortion and the use of human embryos in medicine and other products.[43] In addition, child trafficking and other crimes against humanity remain commonplace among the fourth beast governments.[44]

King Cyrus ultimately faced off with Babylon in two battles. In the first battle, Nabonidus led the Babylonian army to battle with King Cyrus in the battle of Opis. King Cyrus defeated him, leaving Nabonidus' son Belshazzar full king of Babylon. Up to that point, Belshazzar reigned as co-regent under his father. On the open range, King Cyrus defeated Babylon easily. I equate the first battle by King

---

[43] Offit, Paul A. "Vaccine Ingredients – Fetal Cells." *Children's Hospital of Philadelphia*, October 21, 2021. https://www.chop.edu/centers-programs/vaccine-education-center/vaccine-ingredients/fetal-tissues.

[44] Fletcher, Anna. "Government Complacency and Complicity in Human Trafficking." *GlobalJusticeBlog.com*, November 25, 2014. https://law.utah.edu/government-complacency-and-complicity-in-human-trafficking.

Cyrus to President Trump's first term in office. President Trump deflected impeachment efforts, survived assassination attempts and overcame disloyal staff to achieve incredible results in his first term as president. However, he did not "kill Babylon," so to speak.

After Babylon's initial defeat in the battle of Opis, the armies of Babylon then retreated into the impenetrable walls of Babylon (said to be 600 feet tall and 60 feet thick) where they stockpiled enough food and supplies for years. In modern times, Babylon's "walls" include the behemoth private-central-banking finance system that controls nations. It also includes the mainstream media. The modern Babylonian walls include the millions of civil servants bribed and blackmailed to carry out the wishes of the KM (the Khazarian Mafia, the "little horn"). We also know that our government built massive underground bases to survive a nuclear storm using taxpayer money.[45] The modern walls for the deep state are thick and tall.

King Cyrus' momentum stalled after the battle at Opis. He attempted a siege on the huge city of Babylon where King Belshazzar and his men hid. The siege dragged on and King Cyrus began to despair. He then came up with a brilliant plan to divert the Euphrates river feeding the city of Babylon so his men could defeat Babylon *from the inside.* How King Cyrus discovered the plan remains a mystery. Personally, I believe Cyrus discovered himself in the Bible. In Isaiah 44:27, just prior to a verse in which God calls Cyrus by name, the

---

[45]   Klein, Christopher. "Inside the Government's Top-Secret Cold War Hideouts." *History.com*, August 23, 2018. https://www.history.com/news/inside-the-governments-top-secret-doomsday-hideouts.

Bible mentions drying up the rivers. In addition, the prophet Jeremiah commanded his servant Seraiah to read his proclamation warning Babylon of their impending doom and then to drop the scroll to the bottom of the Euphrates River, attached to a rock. No doubt King Cyrus' men discovered the scroll as they marched through the river-bed into Babylon. Some speculate Jeremiah's scroll impacted King Cyrus to the degree that he quickly moved on behalf of Israel after defeating Babylon.

Years earlier, Queen Nitocris, the wife of Nabonidus and the mother of Belshazzar, embarked on an ambitious vanity project to build a bridge over the Euphrates River to connect the two halves of Babylon. Up to this point, people used ferries to cross the river. Her men dug a huge basin to the north, nearly 50 miles in circumference. Using the basin to divert the river, a bridge was constructed of huge stones. However, the basin still remained. King Cyrus used this basin to divert the Euphrates and lower its level enough for King Cyrus' troops to gain access to the city of Babylon. In other words, the structures built by Cyrus' enemies actually gave him the ability to defeat them! I believe this also foreshadows today's battle with Babylon. Soldier Saints will use the fourth beast's infrastructure to bring it down.

In ancient scrolls, the Babylonians admitted they failed to realize King Cyrus began defeating the outskirt cities of Babylon to achieve his objective. Owing to the great size of the city of Babylon, King Cyrus captured the outskirts without the people in the city center knowing. Plus, believing his walls offered complete protection, King Belshazzar arrogantly organized a great feast where he openly mocked God by drinking from the Judean Temple's gold chalices. During the feast, the hand of God wrote on the wall, causing Belshazzar to sober up very quickly! In haste Queen Nitocris summoned the prophet Daniel to interpret the writing on the wall. He delivered this exhortation and interpretation to Belshazzar:

> And you have lifted yourself up against the Lord of heaven, and the vessels of His house have been brought before you, and you and your lords, your wives, and your concubines have drunk wine from them; and you have praised the gods of silver and gold, of bronze, iron, wood, and stone, which do not see or hear or know; but the God in Whose hand your breath is and Whose are all your ways you have not honored and glorified [but have dishonored and disgraced]. Then was the part of the hand sent from the presence of [the Most High God], and this writing was inscribed.
>
> And this is the inscription that was written, MENE, MENE, TEKEL, UPHARSIN—numbered, numbered, weighed, divisions. This is the interpretation of the matter:
>
> MENE, God has numbered the days of your kingship and brought them to an end;
>
> TEKEL, You are weighed in the balances and are found wanting;

> PERES, Your kingdom and your kingship are divided and given to the Medes and Persians (Dan. 5:23-28 AMPC).

God Himself reproves Belshazzar publicly, in front of his friends – a foreshadowing of the coming judgment of the fourth beast. The same evening Babylon fell to King Cyrus and King Darius. Note the inscription on the wall featured "MENE" twice. I believe the inscription contains meaning for our situation today, which I discuss in Chapter 9. I will also explain why I believe the "second battle" of King Cyrus, leading to the total defeat of Babylon rages *right now*, with victory right around the corner.

As King of Persia, people recognized Cyrus as a king of tolerance. He authorized and funded the rebuilding of the Temple in Israel, ultimately allowing Israel to worship in freedom. King Cyrus also respected other religions. The famous Cyrus Cylinder, a 10-inch-long inscribed clay barrel bearing the story of Babylon's "liberation" by Cyrus, tells how Cyrus restored worship at temples where Nabonidus had removed the cult images and brought them to Babylon.[46] While Cyrus acknowledged God and respected the Judean prophets' wisdom and foresight (and strategic help) related to himself, he also respected others' right to worship, and desired to restore other nations' religious customs and return treasure back to where it came from. In the Kingdom Age of the Saints, we are to lead people to Christ, not force them at gunpoint.

---

[46] Fried, Lisbeth S. "Cyrus the Messiah." *Bible Odyssey*. Accessed January 1, 2024. https://open.bibleodyssey.com/articles/cyrus-the-messiah/

Trump, God's "David"

In Kim Clements' prophecies concerning President Trump, he calls him "God's David." Many wrote about King David and his rise to power in the Old Testament. Since Kim's 2014 prophecy, other prophets also refer to President Trump as God's David, including Julie Green. David holds the unique description of "a man after God's own heart" in 1 Samuel 13:14. In perhaps the most famous story in the Bible, David defeated the giant Goliath with a slingshot, helped by the anointing of God. Unlike King Saul and others, David refused intimidation tactics by the mocking giant, instead running *towards* the giant during the take-down, exclaiming:

> You come to me using a sword and two spears. But I come to you in the name of the LORD All-Powerful, the God of the armies of Israel! You have spoken against him. Today the LORD will hand you over to me, and I'll kill you and cut off your head. Today I'll feed the bodies of the Philistine soldiers to the birds of the air and the wild animals. Then all the world will know there is a God in Israel! Everyone gathered here will know the Lord does not need swords or spears to save people. The battle belongs to him, and he will hand you over to us (1 Sam. 17:45-47 NCV).

The passage reveals David knew who he was. He possessed no fear. All the years as a shepherd, learning to meditate on God's word and watching God help him in battles to protect his sheep from the lion, bear and other foes prepared David

78

for this moment. Samuel anointed David king of Israel earlier (1 Sam. 16:13). So David knew God backed him up – he planned to leave the battlefield with Goliath's head.

When I began to hear the prophets refer to President Trump as God's David, it puzzled me at first. I understood the prophecy regarding King Cyrus and President Trump. Cyrus, a flawed and hedonistic leader, fulfilled God's plan but did not know God that we are aware of. On the other hand, David *knew* God. However, there are parallels. Like Trump, David liked women and had multiple wives. David exhibited extreme machismo, as we read in his battle cry to Goliath. Think about it, a scrawny little kid trained as a shepherd faces a towering, nine-foot-plus giant groomed for war and threatens to cut his head off! Pretty brave by all definitions. Prior to the battle, he went around the camp and asked people, "what do I get if I kill him?" He wanted to know the prize, because he fully intended to earn the prize.

Many Christians today would criticize David and call him "arrogant." But in fact, David possessed a righteous indignation that I also observe in Trump. The Israelites standing around the valley, shaking in fear when Goliath taunted them represented the establishment or the status quo. Their king, Saul lost his anointing and God no longer trusted him. Compromise cost Saul his kingdom and now when a real battle faced him, he could no longer hear God's voice. Led by a compromised King Saul, the soldiers camped around the valley also failed to hear God's voice. It took an outsider, a kid who knew who he was and did not play politics to see the situation from 50,000 feet and speak the truth.

In verse 26 of the same chapter, "David asked the men who stood near him, 'What will be done to reward the man who kills this Philistine and takes away the shame from Israel? Who does this uncircumcised Philistine think he is? Does he think he can speak against the armies of the living God'?" In verse 28, his brothers ridiculed him, asking, "Why did you come here? Who's taking care of those few sheep of yours in the desert? I know you are proud and wicked at heart. You came down here just to watch the battle." David's courage and willingness to speak the truth now got him in trouble. You see, David put his finger on the issue. He recognized that Israel's army lost their fight and were now a useless, tired apparatus up against the real enemy.

When President Trump began to do the same thing in Washington by pointing out all the mistakes the Republican party made along the way, it made people uncomfortable. He stepped over the line by accusing President George W. Bush of lying about Iraq and wasting American resources in an ill-conceived war. He went after the military-industrial-complex. In very plain language, he said what Americans were thinking – boldly treading into territory where no other "politician" dared. Trump bitterly spoke of America going to war and "getting nothing for it." When Trump arrived in Washington, he acted a lot like King David showing up at the camp.

King David in the Bible waged war like no other king. He went after the enemies of Israel himself. He got his hands dirty in the fight. When he did not go himself, he made a huge mistake when he fell for another man's wife, Bathsheba (2 Sam. 11). The Bible describes King David relentlessly pursuing the enemies of God with extreme tenacity:

> Later, David attacked and badly defeated the Philistines. Israel was now free from their control.
>
> David also defeated the Moabites. Then he made their soldiers lie down on the ground, and he measured them off with a rope. He would measure off two lengths of the rope and have those men killed, then he would measure off one length and let those men live. The people of Moab had to accept David as their ruler and pay taxes to him.
>
> David set out for the Euphrates River to build a monument there. On his way, he defeated the king of Zobah, whose name was Hadadezer the son of Rehob. In the battle, David captured seventeen hundred cavalry and twenty thousand foot soldiers. He also captured war chariots, but he destroyed all but one hundred of them.
>
> When troops from the Aramean kingdom of Damascus came to help Hadadezer, David killed twenty thousand of them. He left some of his soldiers in Damascus, and the Arameans had to accept David as their ruler and pay taxes to him.
>
> Everywhere David went, the Lord helped him win battles.

Hadadezer's officers had carried their arrows in gold cases hung over their shoulders, but David took these cases and brought them to Jerusalem. He also took a lot of bronze from the cities of Betah and Berothai, which had belonged to Hadadezer.

King Toi of Hamath and King Hadadezer had been enemies. So when Toi heard that David had attacked and defeated Hadadezer's whole army, he sent his son Joram to praise and congratulate David. Joram also brought him gifts made of silver, gold, and bronze. David gave these to the LORD, just as he had done with the silver and gold that he had captured from Edom, Moab, Ammon, Philistia, and from King Hadadezer of Zobah.

David fought the Edomite army in Salt Valley and killed eighteen thousand of their soldiers. When he returned, he built a monument. David left soldiers all through Edom, and the people of Edom had to accept him as their ruler.

Wherever David went, the Lord helped him (2 Sam. 8:1-14 CEV).

David went after the genetically defiled "nephilim" giants with a vengeance. In Moab, David spared the lives of the men that were not "giants," by measuring them with a rope. In all these passages, David brought the spoils of war back home to the Lord. In the Kingdom Age, the spoils of war are distributed to God's people, who will use the resources for the

Lord's work. Twice in the list of battles, the Bible states that the Lord helped David win the battles. I believe another reason God speaks of Trump as His David is because David *himself* went to war against the evil enemies of God and never backed down. President Trump also never retreats. David possessed no fear – He knew God had his back.

I believe one reason Trump represents both a King Cyrus and a King David has to do with his fellowship and relationship with God. I remain convinced that President Trump loves the Lord and likely discovered himself in the Word of God. He probably knows he fulfills Bible prophecy concerning the next age. In future chapters, I will unseal more specific promises related to President Trump in the Bible. Once a man or woman sees themselves in the Word, they begin to enter their high calling and no longer walk in fear or are swayed by the fear of man. Have you discovered yourself in the Bible? Once you do, your whole life changes.

5. False Israel

Take note! I will make those of the synagogue of Satan who say they are Jews and are not, but lie— behold, I will make them come and bow down before your feet and learn and acknowledge that I have loved you.

– Rev 3:9 AMPC

When I began to write on the Kingdom Age of the Saints, I preferred to stick to the wonderful Bible promises and stay away from exposing evil and deception in our world. However, I felt the prompting of the Lord to expose evil to prepare the Body of Christ to become Soldier Saints in the Kingdom Age. You see, Soldier Saints not only know the promises of God, but through discernment are able to spot infiltration and every form of evil. In the Kingdom Age of the Saints, Satan remains unbound. He will use every weapon available as he attempts to regain geopolitical control. God will place the geopolitical control of the world in the hands of awakened Soldier Saints who are not fooled by Satan's deceptions and propaganda.

Jesus spent a significant portion of His earthly ministry teaching His followers about the "sons of the age" – fourth beast controllers who through subtle methods rule the world from behind-the-scenes. Jesus educated His disciples on how to handle snakes and scorpions – the serpent class of evil rulers. Finally, Jesus vehemently rejected the "modern" form of Judaism at the time, the tradition of the elders, embodied by the political life of the Pharisees, the ruling class within the synagogues who called themselves Jews yet were unable to recognize their own Messiah, the very one they taught about.

The Bible foretold the fourth beast's alignment with a false form of Judaism prior to the destruction of the second Judean Temple in AD 70. Ancient Rome hand-picked the Pharisaical leaders during the time of Jesus. In Daniel 11:30 we read he (the fourth beast) shall, "carry out his rage *and* indignation against the holy covenant *and* God's people, and he shall do his own pleasure; and he shall even turn back and make common cause with those [Jews] who abandon the holy covenant [with God]" (AMPC). From the words of Jesus, it's clear He refused to acknowledge the Pharisees as the rightful shepherds of the law of Moses. The Pharisees, the ruling political class in Jesus' day, followed the oral tradition, not the law of Moses.

The tradition of the elders, oral traditions superseding the law of Moses, established a *foothold* in the Judean faith evident during the time of Jesus' ministry. The oral tradition later morphed into a voluminous set of laws and commentary called the Babylonian Talmud, completed circa AD 500. Whereas the Old Testament points toward Jesus as the Messiah, the Talmud contains evil and satanic laws mocking Christians and allowing adherents to commit heinous crimes with no punishment. The Talmud represents the foundational laws of modern Judaism today.[47] Most Christians believe that Jews study the Old Testament and Christians study both the Old Testament and the New Testament. This belief defies reality. Modern Rabbinic Judaism considers the Babylonian Talmud as supreme law. The Talmud teaches that Jews are a superior race and the only purpose of the goyim (non-Jews) is to serve the Jews.[48] It even authorizes theft and pedophilia. Jesus famously rebuked the Pharisees who held to the oral tradition saying, "Their worship is a farce, for they teach man-made ideas as commands from God. For you ignore God's law and substitute your own tradition" (Mark 7:7-8 NLT).

In roughly AD 800, the Khazars (or Khazarians), a mercenary tribe of people who ruled a mighty empire located in what's now known as Ukraine and Kazakhstan, adopted Rabbinic Judaism as their religion. They were not blood descendants of Jacob. When Rus (or Russia) defeated the Khazars' militarily in AD 1000, the Khazars took their tremendous gold and silver reserves and migrated to western Europe. There, the Khazars infiltrated into western society by

---

47 Wikipedia. 2024. "Talmud." Wikimedia Foundation. Last modified December 7, 2024. https://en.wikipedia.org/wiki/Talmud.
48 Freedman, *Facts are Facts,* 70-71.

leveraging past alliances with the Byzantine and Holy Roman Empires and Britain (through marriage or other means) and began controlling *many* venerable institutions and governments.

The Khazars later invented fractional reserve banking and are now shareholders in all private-central-banks in the world. As their power grew, the Khazarians hijacked the Judean religion, brutally killing the real descendants of Jacob at every opportunity. God promised in the book of Revelation that He would preserve a remnant of the blood of the seed of Jacob (see Rev. 12). In my previous book, *KAS*, I identified the Khazarian Jews (abbreviated "KM" or "bankers" in Chapter 2) as the little horn spoken of by the prophet Daniel, a tribe that wields control over the fourth beast by subduing nations using bribery, blackmail, and other nefarious methods.[49]

The State of Israel

Today, Christians confuse the state or government of Israel with God's people of promise in the Bible. Thousands of books written by biblical scholars made predictions related to Christ's return based on the formation date of the modern State of Israel on May 14, 1948. Many thought the formation of the State of Israel constituted a significant prophetic marker in the Bible. Some believed that Jesus would return within a generation, or forty years of the State of Israel's formation, based on Matthew 24:32-34. Literally hundreds of prophetic books written on the subject and making predictions concerning the significance of it proved false –

---

[49]   Thomas, *Kingdom Age of the Saints,* 38, 41-46.

the dates came and went. Is the formation of the State of Israel less significant in the prophetic timeline than we thought?

In the last decade, my eyes opened to many falsehoods I learned in school, saw on the news, or was taught within the evangelical church. This personal "awakening" caused me to rethink everything. From learning new truths about the September 11 attack and watching the media blatantly lie about Donald Trump's involvement with Russia, to finding many of the reasons the United States sent our sons to war false, the "media narratives" no longer ring true for me. When something big *happens*, I tend to *turn* on CNN for a few minutes, take note of the headline, and then explore whether the opposite is true. As a result of a personal awakening, I began to wonder, "Were we also lied to about Israel?"

Recently we watched the State of Israel indiscriminately bomb Palestine where mostly children comprise the populous. Analysis shows that Israel dropped more bombs in the first month of the attack on Palestine than the world observed since the Vietnam War.[50] The headlines say they deserved it and Israeli prime minister Benjamin Netanyahu began recounting the times of Israel in the Bible when Joshua fought and destroyed the Amalekites following God's command. In the Bible, the Amalekites were giants, remnants of the genetically defiled Nephilim. There is a big difference between Amalekites and Palestinian

---

[50]   Qiblawi, Tamara et al. "'Not seen since Vietnam': Israel dropped hundreds of 2,000-pound bombs on Gaza, analysis shows." *CNN*, December 22, 2023. https://www.cnn.com/gaza-israel-big-bombs/index.html

children! Yet the American church dutifully supports the State of Israel, often quoting Genesis 12:3 (ESV), "I will bless those who bless you, and him who dishonors you I will curse, and in you all the families of the earth shall be blessed." This scripture represents a promise God made to Abram when He separated Abram from his relatives and set him apart. Is this verse a command for Christians today to support the government of the nation of Israel?

To answer the question, we must go back to the formation of the modern State of Israel. In 1917, the British Government sent a letter during the First World War to Lord Rothschild, a leader of the British Jewish community, promising a Jewish state in Palestine. The infamous letter became known as the Balfour Declaration.[51] Many believe that commitment was part of a deal to get the United States into the war (World War I) to help Britain win. At the time, the Palestine populous included both Palestinian Muslims (~90%) and Christians (~10%).[52]

It took another few decades for the Balfour Declaration to become reality, aided in large part by the Jewish-controlled media in the United States and the events surrounding World War II, when the persecution of Jews by Hitler was widely publicized. We are led to believe a remnant of the ancient tribes of Israel, the seed of Jacob, reassimilated in Israel and formed a nation. Christians are taught this event was biblical, necessitating unconditional support for the State of the Israel. However, recent and comprehensive genetic studies

---

51 Wikipedia. 2023. "Balfour Declaration." Wikimedia Foundation. Last modified December 11, 2023. https://en.wikipedia.org/wiki/Balfour_Declaration.
52 Wikipedia. 2024. "Palestinian Christians." Wikimedia Foundation. Last modified February 5, 2024. https://en.wikipedia.org/wiki/Palestinian_Christians.

conclude that modern-day Jews are largely descendants of the Khazars and have no genetic markers of the ancient tribes whatsoever.[53] It was discovered by researcher Eran Elhaik of Johns Hopkins University that other published studies to the contrary were essentially "made up."

The Star of David

If the Jews in control of Israel are not blood descendants of Jacob and they observe and recognize as law a commentary (the Babylonian Talmud) that is anti-Christian and based upon an extension of teaching that Jesus called a "farce" in Mark 7:7, should we support them? No, we should not. The more I study the modern form of Rabbinic Judaism and understand its roots, I find it is purely satanic in nature. For instance, the "Star of David," the symbol on the national flag of Israel, is not a divinely inspired symbol. King David did not march into battle using that star. The "Star of David" originated long before it was adopted by the Jewish faith and Zionist movement. It was a popular symbol in pagan traditions, including Islam.[54] It first appeared in Jewish literature in the Babylonian Talmud as an epithet for God. The hexagram (six-pointed star) frequently indicates Saturn worship, as Saturn contains a hexagonal cloud pattern on its north pole.[55] The hexagon is considered a divine symbol by

53   Venton, Danielle. "Highlight: Out of Khazaria–evidence for "Jewish Genome" Lacking." Europe PMC, (2013). Accessed January 16, 2024. https://europepmc.org/article/PMC/3595031.
54   Cohen, Sharon. "The Story of the Star of David." *The Librarians,* May 19, 2021. https://blog.nli.org.il/en/star-of-david/
55   Choi, Charles Q. "Bizarre Giant Hexagon on Saturn May Finally be Explained." *Space,* September 22, 2015. https://www.space.com/30608-mysterious-saturn-hexagon-explained.html

the Freemasons – a symbol of the universal creation or the "seal of Solomon."[56]

Biblical prophets rebuked pagan Jews attempting to adopt the hexagram as their symbol throughout history. In Acts 7:43, Stephen rebuked the Pharisees and recounted Israel taking up the tent of Moloch (a pagan god) in the wilderness and the star of their god Rephan. The prophet Amos prophesied to Israel, "[No] but [instead of bringing Me the appointed sacrifices] you carried about the tent of your king Sakkuth and Kaiwan [names for the gods of the planet Saturn], your images of your star-god which you made for yourselves [and you will do so again]" (Amos 5:26 AMPC). Again, we see the ancient origins of the "Star of David" – essentially pagan worship of the god Saturn. The entire State of Israel's persona is based on deception and Satan worship. It's time for the Church to wake up.

Modern Israel in the Bible

The formation of the modern State of Israel represents a fulfillment of Bible prophecy, but *not* the way the Church taught Christians. The prophet Daniel predicted the modern State of Israel:

> He (the little horn) shall enter into the Glorious Land [Palestine] and many shall be overthrown, but these shall be delivered out of his hand: Edom, Moab, and the main [core] of the people of Ammon. He shall stretch out his hand also against

---

56 "Seal of Solomon." *Masonic Encyclopedia*. Accessed January 2, 2024. https://masonicshop.com/encyclopedia/topics/entry/?i=1713

the [other] countries, but the land of Egypt shall not be among the escaped ones. But he shall have power over the treasures of gold and of silver and over all the precious things of Egypt, and the Libyans and the Ethiopians shall accompany him [compelled to follow his steps] (Dan. 11:41-43).

In this passage, the "he" that enters Palestine represents the little horn – the KM control Palestine! The Rothschild family represents one of the prominent families among the KM. They are named treasurers of the Vatican in the Jewish Encyclopedia.[57] They wielded powerful influence to infiltrate and control the banking industry. Within the Balfour Declaration, it was Lord Rothschild that negotiated with the British to establish the land of Palestine as the Jewish state. Today in modern Israel, 90% of the land of Israel is owned by either the State of Israel, the Development Authority, or the National Jewish Fund, setup by the Rothschilds.[58] The Rothschild family began accumulating the land in Palestine beginning in 1882, and accumulated massive tracts in the region over the next 60 years. Palestinian landowners received pressure to sell from the British Government.[59] If someone wants to own a house in Israel today, they must lease the land from the Rothschilds. Does this sound like the fulfillment of blessing that God ordained for the people of Israel?

57 F. Tupper Saussy, *Rulers of Evil* (n.p.: Ospray, 1999), 160-61.
58 Wikipedia. 2023. "Israeli Land and Property Laws." Wikimedia Foundation. Last modified December 8, 2023. https://en.wikipedia.org/wiki/Israeli_land_and_property_laws.
59 "Rothschild Land Purchases and Early Israel." *Sursock House,* Accessed January 2, 2024. https://sursockhouse.com/rothschild-land-purchases-and-early-israel/

Note in Daniel 11:41-43 that after the little horn takes over Palestine, the little horn then takes over Ethiopia, Egypt and Libya. On the timeline of world events, all three of these nations experienced conflict after the State of Israel formed in 1948 which involved their banking and finance systems. Remember (from Chapter 2) that America serves as a pawn of the little horn, fighting wars on behalf of the bankers, especially against nations operating independent central banks. The Arab and second Arab Springs were coordinated anti-government protests that spread across much of the Arab world beginning in 2010 under the Obama administration. Multiple large-scale conflicts followed, including the Egyptian, Yemeni and Libyan Crises, where regime changes occurred.[60]

Libya transitioned from a beautiful independent nation led by a benevolent King Muamammer Gaddafi, where energy and education was free and the standard of living was high, to an ugly war zone. Like clockwork, a newly-installed private-central-bank went in to control the economy. A virtually identical game plan was instituted in Egypt, whose new central bank floated the Egyptian pound in 2016. The National Bank of Ethiopia was established in 1963 and aided by U.S. State Department emissary Earle O. Latham, who was vice president of the Federal Reserve Bank of Boston.[61]

If the State of Israel is described in Daniel 11:41, then no prophetic significance exists for the current State of Israel. The State of Israel is simply a trophy on the wall of the little

---

[60] Wikipedia. 2024. "Arab Spring." Wikimedia Foundation. Last modified February 4, 2024. https://en.wikipedia.org/wiki/Arab_Spring.
[61] Wikipedia. 2024. "National Bank of Ethiopia." Wikimedia Foundation. Last modified November 18, 2023. https://en.wikipedia.org/wiki/National_Bank_of_Ethiopia.

horn – a Khazarian trojan horse designed to influence American Christians into supporting their wars. When bringing up these points with friends and family, I am often told rehearsed soundbites, like "Israel is the only democracy in the Middle East," or "Israel is our closest ally." First of all, we are talking about a government body that rules the area around Jerusalem. This same government forced its citizens to receive the Covid vaccine at the highest compliance of any nation in the world – 78% of Israelis over the age of 12 are vaccinated.[62] The Covid vaccine is proven to create long term health complications.[63] If the State of Israel is truly "God's chosen government," why are they poisoning their own citizens?

When not behind the cameras, Israel's prime minister repeatedly made derogatory remarks about America. He was once overheard by an ex-CIA agent as saying, "Once we squeeze all we can out of the United States, it can dry up and blow away."[64] In a 2001 video, Netenyahu is quoted as saying, "America is a thing you can move very easily, move it in the right direction."[65] In a 2015 article by the *Forward* magazine, a Jewish paper, the author said, "Israelis tend to agree on one thing: Their strongest supporters (Americans) are an

[62] Estrin, Daniel. "Highly Vaccinated Israel Is Seeing A Dramatic Surge In New COVID Cases. Here's Why." *NPR,* August 20, 2021. https://www.npr.org/sections/goatsandsoda/2021/08/20/1029628471/highly-vaccinated-israel-is-seeing-a-dramatic-surge-in-new-covid-cases-heres-why.

[63] Maucevic, Alexander. Adler, John R. "A Case Report: Long Post-COVID Vaccination Syndrome During the Eleven Months After the Third Moderna Dose." *NIH,* December 12, 2022. https://www.ncbi.nlm.nih.gov/pmc/articles/PMC9833629/

[64] Madsen, Wayne. "The Demise of Global Communications Security." *Online Journal,* September 21, 2005. http://web.archive.org/web/20060512234448/http://www.onlinejournal.org/Special_Reports/092105Madsen/092105madsen.html

[65] "Netanyahu In 2001: 'America Is A Thing You Can Move Very Easily'." *Huffington Post,* May 25, 2011. https://www.huffpost.com/entry/netanyahu-in-2001-america_n_649427

inherently dupable people."[66] I don't know about you, but I don't like being called a *fool*. I think it's time we cut ties with the Khazarian State of Israel. God promised a future for blood descendants of Jacob, not a corrupt state whose existence depends on duping Christians.

Two Types of "Jews"

We need to ask ourselves, "Who are the true Judeans?" True Judeans are the blood descendants of Jacob. God promised in the future to raise up a remnant of the tribes of Israel to do battle with the anti-Christ. These blood descendants of Jacob number 144,000 (Rev 14:1-3). God warns us in Revelation 12 that the dragon (Satan) would attempt to destroy the bloodline of Mary, a descendant of Abraham, Isaac, and Jacob (Luke 3:34, Rev 12).

Numerous attempts were made in recent history to eliminate the bloodline of Jacob. Under the fourth beast, the Judean blood-wars began with the Jewish-Roman Wars, where millions of Judeans were killed.[67] Literally hundreds of other examples of Judean anti-Semitism are chronicled in history. Satan did not care whether he used Romans, Catholics, Spaniards, Khazarian Jews, Nazis, Communists or any other pawn to kill Judeans. He desires the original descendants of Jacob ethnically cleansed. The Khazarian Jews possess a truly remarkable ability to pretend they, not

[66] Zeveloff, Naomi. "What Do Israelis Think About Americans? Start With Disdain." *Forward,* March 8, 2015. https://forward.com/israel/216074/what-do-israelis-think-about-americans-start-with/

[67] Wikipedia. 2023. "Jewish–Roman Wars." Wikimedia Foundation. Last modified December 4, 2023. https://en.wikipedia.org/wiki/Jewish%E2%80%93Roman_wars.

the Judeans, are the victims of ethnic cleansing. However, history reveals the truth. We need to stop falling for the lie.

Today, there are two main groups of people calling themselves Jews. It's critical Christians understand the difference. The first group are the real Jews, whom I call Judeans. These are the blood descendants of Jacob, of the twelve tribes of Israel. Jesus was Judean, of the tribe of Judah (see Matthew 1). Jesus refers to other Judeans as the "lost sheep of Israel" in Matthew 15:24. By calling them lost sheep, Jesus exposes that Judeans' lack a true shepherd. He called the false shepherds, the Pharisees, devouring wolves in sheep's clothing (Matt 7:15). As in Jesus' day, there are many false shepherds calling themselves rabbis today.

The second group of people calling themselves Jews are the Khazarian Jews. These Jews don't descend from Jacob, and instead converted to Judaism based on the Babylonian Talmud as a tribe over 1,200 years ago.[68] King Herod's father Antipater, an Idumean, also "converted" to Judaism. Rome made his son, Herod the Great, the king of the Jewish state at the time of Jesus.[69] We recall Herod tried to kill Jesus at birth. Was Herod's progeny a remnant of "God's chosen people?"

Paul, the Apostle, points out the distinction between the types of Jews, "For some of the Jews killed the prophets, and some even killed the Lord Jesus. Now they have persecuted us, too. They fail to please God and work against all humanity" (1 Thess. 2:15 NLT). Paul didn't overgeneralize – he said "some" of the Jews. Paul declares they "work against

---

[68]   Ankori, Karaites in Byzantium: The Formative Years, 970-1100, (New York: AMS Press, 1968), 64-86.
[69]   Bigland, J. *A Compendious History of the Jews.* (London: 1820), 179.

all humanity." Paul here is talking about the infiltrators like King Herod and his handpicked high priests that adopted the *oral* tradition, not the law of Moses. Today, I believe the Khazarian Jews continue to work against all humanity.

House of Chabad

People recognize the house of Chabad, also known as Lubavitch, Habad and Chabad-Lubavitch as one of the world's best-known Jewish Hasidic movements. It's one of the largest Jewish religious organizations in the world.[70] The sect bases their beliefs on the kabbalistic "tree of life." The Kabbalah is part of the oral law and a mystical interpretation contained within the Babylonian Talmud.

In January 2024, a video surfaced of a police raid of the Chabad headquarters in Brooklyn, NY. In the video, police discovered a tunnel system in the walls of the Chabad synagogue. Later, videos surfaced where detectives followed the tunnels to reveal a massive underground tunnel system. The exposure of the hidden tunnels under Chabad headquarters revealed child seats, blood-stained child mattresses, blood-stained rags and a Mikveh (ritual bathhouse). An anonymous source explained the use of a Mikveh bath:

> A Mikveh bath is used to immediately purify oneself after experiencing 'keri,' or ejaculation. According to the Torah, bathing in a Mikveh is

---

required before being allowed to eat a "terumah," or a "Korban" (slaughtered sacrificial offering).[71]

According to another New York based source, the tunnel discovered under the Chabad headquarters connects to a network that "runs all over the city to strategic locations, including the local Children's Museum." The source believed the tunnels were used in child trafficking and Adrenochrome production.

Adrenaline harvesting from the blood of terrorized children produces Adrenochrome. As a chemical, its supposed benefits are well documented.[72] The mainstream media vilifies the discussion of Adrenochrome as "conspiracy theory." The horrors of Adrenochrome production defy human comprehension. However, now that police videos confirm the existence of child torture chambers in tunnels, we should pay attention to all previously labeled "conspiracy theories" related to Adrenochrome production and child sacrifice.

Journalist Richard Potcner analyzed the video of the Chabad synagogue raid and pointed out that the rabbis attempted to corner the police conducting the raid by erecting barriers formed with pews to entrap the police.[73] Richard's analysis makes it clear that the tunnel raid probably happened before, only the police in prior raids

[71]   Fulford, Benjamin. "Chabad human sacrifice exposed as Europe revolts and Texas declares civil war." January 15, 2024. https://benjaminfulford.net/chabad-human-sacrifice-exposed-as-europe-revolts-and-texas-declares-civil-war/

[72]   "Adrenochrome." *National Institute of Health,* Accessed January 30, 2024. https://pubchem.ncbi.nlm.nih.gov/compound/Adrenochrome

[73]   "An RCJ Play by Play Breakdown of the at Times Violent Confrontation between NYPD and Hasidic Jews at the Chanda Headquarters in New York." Richardcitizenjournalists. January 17, 2024. Video, https://t.me/Richardcitizenjournalists.

likely *did* not make it ou*t*. The videos show n*o* backup came to assist the NYPD cops performing the raid.

The gritty underworld of the house of Chaba*d* should raise additional red flags for Christians who blindly support the Jews as "God's chosen pe*o*ple." I firml*y* believe there are millions of Jews that don't participate in vile acts of the Chabad, and are like other lost souls longing for a relationship with God. Christians should continue to reach *these* Jews with the Gospel of Jesus Christ. Jesus also came for the lost sheep of the house of Israel (Matt 15:24).

Esau's Blessing

Esau's father Isaac gave his second-born son Jacob a blessing he originally intended for his first-born son, Esau. Jacob deceived his father (with the help of his mother, Rebekah) to obtain the coveted first-born blessing. I believe God orchestrated the event, as Esau despised his birthright. Isaac's blessing of Esau prophesied hatred between the brothers' seed:

> You will live away from the richness of the earth, and away from the dew of the heaven above. You will live by your sword, and you will serve your brother. But when you decide to break free, you will shake his yoke from your neck (Gen. 27: 39-40).

Esau, the red child, developed a root of bitterness after Jacob stole his birthright. Some scholars believe the root of bitterness in Esau paved the way to unzip Nephilim genes in

Esau's bloodline.[74] Esau's seed *did* decide to break free from Jacob's "yoke." The tribe of Amalek were the product of Esau's descendants and became arch-enemies to the Israelites, the seed of Jacob. After the Kingdoms of Israel and Judah fell, the seed of Jacob lived in total subjection to pagan empires until the present day. Esau broke free from Jacob's yoke, as his father prophesied.

Jacob's birth constituted a sign of the end of the present age. Jacob came out of the womb gripping the heel of Esau (Gen. 25:26). The Lord explains the significance in 2 Esdras:

> He said to me, "From Abraham to Isaac, because from him were born Jacob and Esau, for Jacob's hand held Esau's heel from the beginning. Now Esau is the end of this age, and Jacob is the beginning of the age that follows (2 Esdras 6:8-9 NRSV).

Esau leads the end of the current age. Esau represents the child who hated the birthright and instead chose evil by choosing to satisfy carnal needs rather than standing firm on who God called him to be. But what is God speaking of when He declares the seed of Jacob is the beginning of the new age? Of course, Jesus descended from Jacob, through Judah. However, Jesus' birth and resurrection did not birth the next age. Jesus came 2,000 years *before* the next age, as I cover in later chapters. As we begin the new age, beginning with the Kingdom Age of the Saints, I believe God reveals the true seed of Jacob to humanity. We will discover many influential

---

[74] Sanger, Laura. *The Roots of the Federal Reserve: Tracing the Nephilim from Noah to the US Dollar.* (Dallas: Relentlessly Creative Books, 2020). 167.

Soldier Saints, possibly even President Trump, descend from Jacob's seed.

The Judean's Future

According to Revelation 12, God no longer needs to *protect* the ethnic Judeans after the dea*th* of the fourth beast. In Revelations 12:14, the Bible says the woma*n* (carrier of the bloodline of Jacob) i*s* afforded protec*tion* and kept safe for a time, and times, and half a time. This time frame matches the len*g*th of the lease of the fou*r*th be*a*st, which is 2,150 years.[75] The fourth beast's reign ends and then geopolitical control of the *w*orld passes to the sai*n*ts during the Kingd*o*m Age. Than*kfu*lly, the Kingdom Age of the Saints ushe*r*s in a *t*ime of peace for the Judeans. This tells me God plans a great exposure and subsequent defeat of the false Is*r*ael, currently run by the Khazarian Jews.

---

[75]   Thomas, *Kingdom Age of the Saints*, 68.

6. Two Presidents?

But Zadok the priest, Benaiah the son of Jehoiada, Nathan the prophet, Shimei, Rei, and David's most formidable warriors did not side with Adonijah [in his desire to become king].

– 1 Kings 1:8 AMPC

In November 2020, a patriotic media-powerhouse walked into President Trump's office and laid out a plan to "re-win" the election. Trump supposedly "lost" the election in the wee-hours of November 4, 2020 and most people smelled a rat. This person knew how to harness President Trump's strengths to regain the momentum and pressure the state legislators into looking more carefully into the machinations and fraud. This individual could make it happen for President Trump assuming access to a financial war-chest. President Trump listened intently to the plan. He then said, "We don't have the money" and ended the meeting.

Mike Lindell of the My Pillow company also made a trip to the White House. We all remember the closeup photographs of Mike Lindell's notes taken by a *Washington Post* photographer. Mike clearly visited the White House to discuss declaring martial law and a state-of-emergency to defend the Constitution. Mike later recounted his meeting with President Trump. The outcome for Mike proved similar to that of President Trump's first visitor.

Finally, Sidney Powell took a shot. She certainly had the legal credibility. On her own dime, she filed many lawsuits and seemed to grasp the particulars of election law very well. I imagine President Trump appreciated her efforts, but she also recounts a lack of action by Trump.

Did President Trump simply give up? After months of warning patriots across America that the Democrats planned to steal the election, why wasn't President Trump more prepared? And the Republican National Committee's (the RNC) response represented classic D.C. politics, "Here you go, Trump... Here's $200 million... Hire a good legal team and good luck." Meanwhile, the RNC passed up numerous opportunities to shore up their voter-registration database, or even conduct training sessions with state legislators, etc. I learned from a source who worked at the RNC that it was recommended years before the 2020 election the RNC invest in a digital-warehouse with voter rolls, aligned with machine-learning algorithms to prepare for the "big steal." Instead of acting on the smart proposal, they fired the person who recommended the proposal along with their whole team of data scientists! The RNC either exhibited gross negligence or wanted President Trump to lose. Over the years, the RNC apparently learned they get more donations when they are the underdog. When you win, you actually have to pass laws and do work. It's much easier to be the losing party and sit back with a box of Cheetos and loudly bemoan outrage at the Democrats!

Personally, I knew the battle was over as I listened to Mark Levin on *Patriot Radio* just after the election in November 2020. A state legislator from Pennsylvania called the toll-free number advertised on Levin's show, told Mark who she was, and then asked, "What should I do?" I thought to myself, "Whoa, this is a bad sign." If the state legislators in the swing states were not briefed along the way to expect election shenanigans and provided with an outline of how to respond, maybe all was lost. Sure enough, President Trump's legal team lacked the data and legal files to win cases, the state legislators operated out of step, and President Trump's VP Pence seriously dropped the ball on January 6.

The Die-Hards

Up until January 20, 2021, quite a few of us still believed a miracle would happen. Admittedly, we probably over-internalized our interpretations of the "Trump prophecies." For weeks and almost on a daily basis, analysts like Mike

Adams from *Brighteon Broadcast News* would list "Trump's remaining options." Many prophets, such as Robin Bullock and Hank Kunneman, repeatedly reiterated they felt certain that President Trump would move into a second term.

Simultaneously, a handful of die-hards working in the Trump administration worked tirelessly to install safeguards around key Trump policies such as the border wall to prevent the next administration from tearing it down. Most of these individuals worked up until their emails were turned off on the morning of January 20, 2021. However, many in the Trump administration had already ejected themselves in mid-late November or early December just to secure income and then "wait it out." The die-hards tasted a *real* momentum-movement to save America underway and did not want it to end. Many senior level Trump appointees felt like things began to accelerate in the last year of the Trump presidency towards real progress, and real change. The early "Bushies" (Bush appointees who largely opposed Trump's agenda), now "Siberia'd" (pushed into a role with no authority), paved the way for real progress.

January 20, 2021 came and the die-hards assembled on the tarmac at Andrews Air Force Base to see President Trump depart. The sound system blared a custom playlist we were told President Trump picked out himself. President Trump thanked the die-hards for their work. There were tears in the eyes of President Trump and Melania as they spoke to the rather small group of a couple-hundred-or-so attendees. While I was there, I noticed a volley of cannon fire off to my right. I remember thinking, why so much cannon fire? The cannon fire came every couple of seconds, and there were four cannons and a large lineup of military personnel conducting the salute. Later, I realized Trump received a full 21-gun salute down to the exact detail, conducted by the 3rd U.S. Infantry Regiment's (The Old Guard) 1st Battalion, the Presidential Salute Battery.

With my family in tow, we tried to re-enter Washington D.C. and discovered all the roads blocked. We talked our way in however, and returned home. Unable to resist, I turned on the mainstream news and watched the "inauguration" of Joseph Biden. I wasn't quite sure at the time, but something seemed very wrong with the inauguration itself. Joe Biden supposedly received 85 million votes, but there was virtually no one in the crowd. Primarily, the crowd included military personnel, possibly National Guard. I remember seeing Joe Biden's motorcade moving past a group of military personnel who turned their backs to him as he drove by, an offense worthy of courts-martial. Being the son of a U.S. military officer, and also knowing many in the military, I knew something strange just occurred on a day that became more surreal by the moment.

A Year of Prayer

As an entrepreneur, I went through cycles of creating companies over many years and then selling them. Usually after a sale, I experienced downtime as I looked for the next venture. My most recent business sale occurred nearly two years before the election. I went through a phase of cranking out new business plans but failing to feel inspiration in my work. Finally, I went to God and felt like my #1 focus should be praying for the nation. So for the next 14 months or so, I prayed for the United States and President Trump for two-to-three hours per day, leading up to January 20, 2021. After witnessing President Trump's "last day," I again knelt to pray for our nation. In my mind, I thought instead of *two-to-three* hours a day of prayer, I needed to pray *four-to-five* hours! In the natural, it *looked* bad. Frankly, it appeared all lost for America.

If a man who campaigned from his basement could win an election in the wee-hours of the morning after November 3, it meant our election system suffered an irredeemable level of corruption. On the campaign trail in 2020, Joe Biden said: "We have put together the most extensive and inclusive voter fraud organization in the history of American politics."[76] It's one of the very few times Biden actually told the truth. At that time, I used to tell people, "nothing shocks me anymore." I found what happened both shocking and disgusting, and realized America suffered far more corruption than I ever considered possible.

Nevertheless, as I knelt down to pray on January 21, 2021, I felt the Spirit of God say, "You don't need to pray anymore, I have this *handled.*" I felt an overwhelming peace come over me. My mind scanned my internal biblical search engine for an explanation and came back with "no results." However, I knew the answer must be in the Bible and so I began to search for it. Up to that point, my knowledge of End

---

[76] "Biden Quotes: Was This The Ultimate Freudian Slip? Biden Says Democrats Built the Largest Voter Fraud Organization in American History." *Coal Region Canary,* November 12, 2020. https://coalregioncanary.om/2020/11/12/joe-biden-quote-voter-fraud-organization/

Times teaching was comprised of hearsay and jumbled commentary with no firm scriptural foundation of my own. I began to seek the scriptures and pray. In December 2022, something happened: God unsealed the books of Daniel and Revelation to me and I began to understand why I possessed supernatural peace.

I learned that *what* happened with Joe Biden needed to happen. The world needed to wake up to the depraved condition of our corrupt government. Our *society* needed to lose its faith in all institutions and seek the Lord in earnest. God's divine plan called for a "Great Awakening"; Awakening to the corruption and matrix that enslaved *humanity*. President Trump interrupted the matrix and therefore he needed to be moved out of the way in their opinion. However, society recognized the glitch in the matrix.

Trump and the Vaccine

After January 2021, Trump remained silent for a bit. In part, President Trump needed to stay quiet because an impeachment hearing went on *after Trump left office.* Thankfully the hearings went nowhere and Trump was acquitted in February 2021. The January 6 "insurrection" dominated the news cycle and the prolonged media hysteria and hype created a smokescreen of ignorance rising to the level where Democrats thought they could actually impeach a person no longer serving as President – a novel concept indeed. The FBI began indiscriminately arresting anyone associated with the January 6 protest – elderly couples, church group leaders and disabled veterans all proved worthy targets for the FBI. They broke down doors and brought in SWAT teams, seeking to scare their prey into heart attacks if at all possible. The deep state sent a message to ordinary Americans: "It's our country and don't you forget it!"

Certainly, the U.S. government possessed several advantages over ordinary Americans. They carried bigger guns and controlled the "Justice" Department. They went after anyone associated with President Trump, including: Roger Stone, Rudy Giuliani, Sydney Powell, Mike Lindell, Jeffrey Clark, Lin Wood and many others. For many of these individuals, their personal nightmares began on January 21, 2021.

While the election and January 6 dominated the headlines in early 2021, another newsworthy enigma began to slowly make its way to the surface. The Covid-19 shots were causing serious health problems. Those that rushed out to receive the shots and especially the people that received multiple boosters began to face deadly complications.[77] President Trump during his presidency remained mostly neutral and made it clear receiving the jab remained a personal decision. However, in 2021 President Trump began to openly endorse the jab. The following are a list of quotes from President Trump regarding the vaccine in 2021:

- **February:** "Everybody, go get your shot."
- **March:** "I would recommend it to a lot of people... it's a safe vaccine, and it's something that works."

---

[77] "Selected Adverse Events Reported after COVID-19 Vaccination." *CDC,* September 12, 2023. https://www.cdc.gov/coronavirus/2019-ncov/vaccines/safety/adverse-events.html

- **Mid-April:** After the *federal* government paused its authorization of the Johnson & Johnson vaccine, Trump said "The federal pause on the J&J shot makes no sense." He went on to say, "This moronic move is a gift to the anti-vax movement... The science bureaucrats are fueling that deranged pseudoscience."

- **Late-April:** "I'm all in *favor* of the vaccine. It's *one* of the great achievements, a *true* miracle, and not only for the United States. We're saving *tens* of millions of lives throughout the world. We're saving entire countries. The vaccine is a great thing, and people should take advantage of it."

- **July:** "I recommend you take it, but I also believe in your freedoms 100 percent."

- **Mid-August:** "Once you get the vaccine, you get better."

- **Late-August:** "Take the vaccines... It is working."

- **September:** "The vaccines do work... And they are effective. So here's my thing: I think I saved millions of lives around the world."

- **December:** "Don't let libs win when you promote vaccine skepticism."[78]

Quietly, a storm brewed in President Trump's voter-base. Each month in 2021, more data and stories emerged detailing horrific medical issues related to receiving the Covid vaccine. Texas cardiologist Dr. Peter McCullough and vaccine scientist Dr. Robert Malone began to share painful truths about how

---

[78] Blake, Aaron. "Dear Republicans: Your favorite president wants you to get vaccinated." *Washington Post,* December 21, 2021.
https://www.washingtonpost.com/politics/2021/12/21/dear-republicans-trump-wants-you-get-vaccinated-thats-not-fake-news/

the Covid-19 vaccine kills. Each month, more data came out and yet, like clockwork, Trump continued to endorse the jab. Alex Jones, who remained a staunch defender of President Trump, famously came out and pulled his endorsement in 2022, chiefly over the Covid-19 vaccine. (Jones since jumped back on the Trump train.)

At every political conference, the subject of Trump's continued endorsement of a poisonous jab became a topic of conversation. It seemed obvious to everyone *but* Trump that he began to lose his support-base. People recounted that Trump's son Baron suffered from Autism, which Trump in previous years attributed to vaccines. In 2014, Trump tweeted, "Healthy young child goes to doctor, gets pumped with massive shot of many vaccines, doesn't feel good and changes – AUTISM. Many such cases!"[79] How could he now blindly overlook the evidence concerning the Covid-19 vaccine?

We all knew Trump hated apologies, but this was different – people were dying. I buried a close (and young) friend in 2022 that dropped dead from a heart attack right in front of his young daughter just a few months after receiving the Covid shot, with no co-morbidities or family history of heart attacks. My friend left a heartbroken wife and three young children behind. For Trump to endorse the shots after witnessing the irreparable harm remained unforgivable for a lot of people.

---

[79]   Carlson, Adam. "Trump Celebrates Autism Awareness Day ... After Years of Falsely Claiming Vaccines Cause Autism." *People*, April 2, 2019. https://people.com/politics/donald-trump-autism-awareness-day-vaccines-tweet/

A person approached me for advice as he considered running for president of the United States and asked me about President Trump's weakness in the upcoming election. Without hesitation, I told them, "The jab." President Trump, who effectively tapped the psyche of the American people in 2016 and promised to bury the deep state in his inaugural speech, now appeared to be part of the deep state, mostly because of his endorsement of the lethal Covid jab. Many of us struggled with questions and many theories emerged. Was President Trump compromised? Was *he* siding with the deep state out of concern for the safety of his family? Was President Trump's inner circle purposely burying him? Was this even the same guy?

Fat-Trump, Skinny-Trump

After President Trump alienated supporters from his base by endorsing the Covid-19 vaccines, another theory emerged from journalist Benjamin Fulford. Benjamin Fulford formerly served as the Asia-Pacific Bureau Chief for *Forbes* magazine and then broke off as an independent journalist and author. Each week, he publishes a video on *rumble.com* and also issues a subscription newsletter and articles on *benjaminfulford.net*. Fulford, famous for his commentary and analysis on the KM, delivers gripping behind-the-scenes analysis of high-level state meetings and tracks which nations continue to align with the KM. Fulford claims he built a list of contacts over many decades that share with him, on an anonymous basis, the inner workings of international governments and intelligence agencies. Fulford appears to split time between Canada and Japan and often his analysis centers on Canadian or Japanese politics. After I was shown by the Lord the KM as the deceitful and evil little horn, the controller of the Rome-rooted fourth beast system, I became especially interested in Fulford's weekly programs as he remains one of the few journalists exposing the KM by name and tracking their moves.

Usually on his weekly videos, Fulford leaves time for subscriber questions and answers (Q&A). Beginning in late 2021 significant questions surfaced around President Trump's stance on vaccines. As a result, Fulford and many others wrote off President Trump as "damaged goods." However, Fulford recently made a *sensational* claim regarding President Trump. According to Fulford, an intelligence source told him the *real* President Trump moved himself and his family to Cheyenne Mountain years ago for safety reasons and to wage a dangerous war on the deep state, aided by the U.S. military and other military forces.

Conversely, the Trump in Mar-Lago represented a compromised body-double controlled by a Freemason named Leo Digami (sp.?).[80] Fulford claimed one could tell the difference by the physique. The compromised Trump "body double" is overweight with sagging jowls and whites under his eyes. Fulford claims the "Fat-Trump" (referring to his large stomach) was rarely seen with Melania Trump and likely served at the behest of the KM as paid opposition, with

---

80   "Benjamin Fulford Update Today January 5, 2024."
     Bitchute.Com/Channel/HTLMmLHA2jeM/. January 5, 2024. Video, 0:11:45,
     https://www.bitchute.com/video/BkJu3q0r0uIh/.

the express goal of destroying President Trump's reputation in the 2024 election.

According to Fulford, the "Skinny-Trump" living in Cheyenne Mountain is the real President Trump. His face and figure are fit and he regularly appears with the real Melania Trump. Fulford suggests at the right time, the "Skinny-Trump" may emerge but only after the last remnants of the deep state are eradicated. Wow! Quite a theory, right?

The Cheyenne Mountain Complex is a United States Space Force installation and defensive bunker located in El Paso County, Colorado near Colorado Springs.[81] Literally carved out of a mountain, the hardened military base was originally constructed during the Cold War to survive a nuclear attack and provide a command post for a U.S. president or other high-ranking military official to facilitate military operations in the event of nuclear war. The facility, built under 2,000 feet of granite, was designed to be self-sufficient for many years. The famous movie, *WarGames*, starring Matthew Broderick, is set partly at the command center in the Cheyenne Mountain Complex.[82] The facility used to be open to the public for tours, but these were shut down in 1999.

I often tell people, "unless I see something in the Bible, I don't believe it." Of course, I am referring to interpreting future world events. For years I complained about the Q-movement because I thought the "trust the plan" component gave people false hope. However, in December 2022, I

[81] Wikipedia. 2024. "Cheyenne Mountain Complex." Wikimedia Foundation. Last modified January 28, 2024.
https://en.wikipedia.org/wiki/Cheyenne_Mountain_Complex.
[82] Badham, John, director. *WarGames*. MGM/UA Entertainment, 1983. 1 hr., 54 min.

discovered the Bible laid out a future quite similar to the one Q described.

I did not buy a single blockchain-based digital asset until I discovered blockchain in the book of Revelation. I ignored the "Q-hopium" because I thought that it gave people false hope until I saw hope for the future in the Bible. When I first heard Fulford's "Fat-Trump, Skinny-Trump" theory, I also dismissed it as one of many theories circulating about Trump and his newly formed endorsement of medical tyranny. However, recently I discovered a peculiar prophecy that I believe pertains to President Trump in the Bible, which caused me to seriously consider Fulford's theory. I talk about this discovery in Chapter 10.

God's Breadcrumbs

Years ago, I met a fascinating man who created the wildly popular video game *Ultima*, Richard Garriott.[83] Richard described how he invented a new "elf language" for *Ultima* and how the game's success related to the hundreds of clues in the game which players needed to solve to reach the credits screen (the end of the game). So called "fantasy computer games" also involve elaborate puzzles, riddles, and hidden clues that keep players engaged.

There are also real-life scavenger hunts. In one famous example, a gentleman named Forrest Fenn buried a box of treasure, worth over one million dollars in the Rocky Mountains and released a riddle as a clue. Whoever found the box could keep it. Thousands-upon-thousands searched

---

[83] Garriott, Richard. *Ultima*. Origin Systems & Electronic Arts. Multiple Platforms. 1981-2013.

for the treasure. Fenn occasionally released additional clues and ten years later someone found the treasure at last![84]

In addition, Hollywood released hundreds of movies where the main character searches for hidden treasure. The fascination that humanity possesses about finding hidden treasure comes from God! I am learning the Bible contains buried clues, riddles and even puzzles that the Lord delights in His children discovering. As I dig into the Word of God, I am amazed how sometimes a seemingly insignificant verse may cast additional meaning or color upon other verses.

In Chapter 4, I share how the prophet Jeremiah released a prophecy about the destruction of Babylon and told his servant to drop the scroll containing the prophecy into the Euphrates River, tied to a rock. King Cyrus' men would certainly discover the scroll, but only after they diverted the Euphrates to gain entrance to Babylon covertly. God dropped a clue as to how to get into Babylon in Isaiah 44:27 (drying up the river) right before He addressed Cyrus by name in the next verse.

In my previous book, *KAS*, I discovered how God hid the details on life during the Kingdom Age of the Saints in a riddle in the book of Revelation. God *loves* riddles and leaves clues and "breadcrumbs" all over the Bible for His saints to find! Have any of you solved the riddle in *KAS*?

---

[84] Greene, Ryan. "3 Mind-Blowing Real-Life Scavenger Hunts." *Watson Adventures,* June 8, 2020. https://watsonadventures.com/blog/fun-stuff/3-mind-blowing-real-life-scavenger-hunts/

Funeral for the Deep State?

On January 20, 2021, Joe Biden was inaugurated as the 46th president of the United States and commander in chief of the U.S. military – or was *he*? I was in Washington D.C. on this *strange* day. I personally witnessed a fiery 21-gun salute for President Trump on the tarmac at Andrews Air Force Base, carried out with ultimate precision. In an unprecedented display, Trump received a 21-gun salute accompanied by a red-carpet ceremony as an *outgoing* U.S. president. Odd.

A January 18, 2021 headline read, "Pentagon REJECTS President's request for huge military-style farewell parade with crowd of supporters hours before Biden's inauguration."[85] A media firestorm erupted and pundits called President Trump "vain and delusional." They excoriated President Trump for his request and euphorically celebrated when supposedly the Pentagon turned down the request. The headline proved to be fake-news, as President Trump got his 21-gun salute and ceremony. It also revealed to the public a rare divide within the military. Given the shenanigans in the 2020 election, many wondered if (and fervently hoped) the military might intervene in some way.

Biden received no 21-gun salute directly after being "sworn in," an unusual omission. Easily available online are videos showing 21-gun salutes immediately following the inaugurations of past U.S. presidents. However, later on inauguration day at approximately 3:00 PM at Arlington

---

85 Caralle, Katelyn. "Pentagon REJECTS President's request for huge military-style farewell parade with crowd of supporters hours before Biden's inauguration." *DailyMail,* January 18, 2021. https://www.dailymail.co.uk/news/article-9156861/Pentagon-denies-Donald-Trumps-request-military-style-farewell-parade.html

National Cemetery Biden, Harris, Obama, Bush, Clinton and their spouses participated in a ceremonial wreath-laying at the Tomb of the Unknown Soldier.[86] According to Arlington National Cemetery's website, a wreath-laying ceremony by a president of the United States typically marks the national observance of Memorial Day or Veterans Day.[87] A wreath-laying is *not* conducted during a presidential inauguration.

According to law, the outgoing U.S. president transitions power at 12:00 Noon (Eastern time) on January 20. But wait, by 3:00 PM on January 20, Biden should be directing the U.S. military as commander in chief, right? The military provided a 21-gun salute for Biden at the ceremony at Arlington National Cemetery. However, the salute itself proved *very* different than President Trump's salute earlier that morning. In President Trump's salute the military fired each volley with an exact *two-second* interval between cannon fires. The battery of cannons during Trump's salute contained *four* cannons, consistent with his inauguration ceremony in 2017 both in terms of the number of cannons and the firing intervals. In contrast, the cannon fire at Arlington National Cemetery went off with *nine-second* intervals with *three* cannons. The soldiers did not arrive in formation, but appeared to be casually standing around before starting the salute.

[86]   Naylor, Brian. "President Biden And Predecessors Attend Wreath-Laying Ceremony At Arlington Cemetery." *NPR,* January 20, 2021.
https://www.npr.org/sections/inauguration-day-live-updates/2021/01/20/958862602/president-biden-and-predecessors-attend-wreath-laying-ceremony-at-arlington-ceme

[87]   "Wreath Layings." *Arlington National Cemetery,* Accessed January 6, 2024.
https://www.arlingtoncemetery.mil/Visit/Events-and-Ceremonies/Wreath-Layings

According to an article published on the Arlington National Cemetery's website, the nine-second interval cannon fire with three cannons is typical of 21-gun salutes held at the cemetery for visits from foreign heads-of-state.[88] The ceremonial wreath-laying on January 20, 2021, conducted for the three former presidents and Joe Biden, was the exact ceremony provided to *foreign dignitaries* paying formal respects to the sacrifices of America's veterans by placing a wreath before the Tomb.

Who ordered this ceremony? If you look at the *footage* of the ceremony, it appeared Bush, Obama, and Clinton *knew* something was wrong. They kept looking around and seemed nervous.[89] Moreover, Taps was played near the end of the ceremony, typical of funerals, wreath-laying and memorial services. Either the military on its own or President Trump gave the order to conduct the wreath-laying ceremony for Biden and the three former presidents. Giving Biden, Obama, Bush and Clinton a ceremony reserved for foreign powers and forcing them to honor the lives of service members lost in wars they foisted on the American people represented THE BIGGEST INSULT TO THE LARGEST GROUP OF FORMER U.S. PRESIDENTS IN AMERICAN HISTORY! There is *no way* Biden would have ordered the ceremony.

If President Trump, who never conceded the 2020 election, acts as the commander in chief of the U.S. military

[88] Hymel, Kevin M. "Presidential Salute Battery Honors Dignitaries and Events." *Arlington National Cemetery,* December 27, 2022. https://www.arlingtoncemetery.mil/Blog/Post/12870/Presidential-Salute-Battery-Honors-Dignitaries-and-Events

[89] "WATCH LIVE: Biden and Harris Families Lay Wreath at Arlington National Cemetery." Youtube.Com/@PBSNewsHour. January 20, 2021. Video, https://www.youtube.com/watch?v=-jtdQGYLD0k.

and Biden acts as president of the United States Corporation, then we do have two presidents, a fulfillment of Kim Clement's prophecy in 2008.

7. The Lion From the Forest

When I looked, I saw what seemed to be a lion roused from the forest, roaring, and I heard how it uttered a human voice to the eagle, and spoke...
– 2 Esdras 11:37 NRSV

The Bible contains many incredible prophecies regarding the future of mankind. These prophecies are so detailed it's hard for some to believe they were written thousands of years ago. I discovered that both Daniel and Revelation describe many End Times events with varying degrees of detail. The book of 2 Esdras provides additional fine-grained detail, particularly regarding how the fourth beast system falls apart.

The Eastern Orthodox Church and some Catholic Bibles contain the book of 2 Esdras. When the Pilgrims traveled across the Atlantic Ocean, they carried *The Geneva Bible* with them. On the Pilgrims' journey, they were *in the act* of fulfilling prophecies outlined in 2 Esdras. *The Geneva Bible* includes 2 Esdras, as do the original versions of the King James Bible and the Revised (and New) Revised Standard Editions. Unfortunately, modern evangelical versions of the Bible do not feature 2 Esdras, although they do contain the book of Ezra, written by the same prophet.

As I began to unseal the books of Daniel and Revelation, I sensed I needed to study the book of 2 Esdras for additional clues concerning our times. Two Esdras contains a remarkable, parallel version to Daniel's interpretation of King Nebuchadnezzar's dream found in Daniel chapter 2.

In Daniel 2, King Nebuchadnezzar, the king of Babylon, had a nightmare that troubled his spirit. He demanded the wise men of the day both recount and interpret the dream. When they failed in this request, the king began killing all the wise men of Babylon. Eventually his troops sought out Daniel and his companions to kill them as well. Daniel approached the king to ask for time to seek the interpretation of the troubling dream. Daniel's request was granted by the king and he returned to his companions and instructed them to seek the Lord for mercy. Daniel was given a dream that night revealing the king's dream and its interpretation. He thanked and blessed the God of Heaven and then went to speak with the king. Daniel not only recounted the dream but also translated the dream for the king.

Daniel received a vision from God showing him what the king dreamed about – a 60 cubit by 6 cubit statue, made up of four different metals. The *golden* head of the statue represented Babylon, the current pagan kingdom at that time. The silver chest and arms represented the next secular empire, Medo-Persia. The bronze belly and thighs represented the third empire, Greece. The iron legs and feet made from iron mixed with clay represented Rome. In Daniel's vision, a heavenly stone pulverized the entire statue by striking the feet first, and that stone then grew into a mountain that covered the earth, an event called the Stone Judgment.

In *KAS*, I explain the vision in greater detail and provide additional background on each pagan kingdom. I also explain how today we live in the time of the fourth secular empire originating in ancient Rome. While ancient Rome fell, Rome itself revived and eventually morphed into the Holy Roman Empire and continued to develop into what is now a league of diverse nations carrying out the satanic agenda of the fourth beast. In the Bible, the fourth beast contains 10 horns (nations), three of which are subdued and controlled by a deceptive little horn.

World control currently falls within the tight grip of the little horn (the KM), which uses the military, financial, and religious might of three powerful nations as the bedrock of control for the world. The grasp of the little horn loosens as I write this book. The more society wakes up to the powerful forces controlling the world, the less these forces can hold onto control. Secret societies thrive on, well – staying secret. Aldous Huxley once said, "A really efficient totalitarian state would be one in which the all-powerful executive of political bosses and their army of managers control a population of slaves who do not have to be coerced, because they love their servitude."[90] This quote aptly describes the modern system the world endures and the all-powerful executive is the KM. The "efficient totalitarian state" can only be executed if society never sees the wizard behind the curtain – but they need a reason to look.

The Covid pandemic caused many to wake up to the close collaboration between the government, corporations, and even religion to achieve tyranny. Society began to become more curious and pay attention, beginning the death process for the fourth beast handlers. But how does the game end for the fourth beast? The book of 2 Esdras gives us an additional page of God's blueprint of how everything unravels for the fourth beast system society currently endures.

Three Subdued Nations

According to the Bible, the little horn subdues three of the ten nations in the fourth beast system with *no army*. The little horn conquers kingdoms in times of peace. "Subdue" means "to subjugate, bring under control, to conquer." Daniel 7:8 (KJV) states "there came up...another little horn, before whom there were three of the first horns plucked up by the roots." Nations subdued by the little horn lose their foundation and instead become subjected to and directed by the little horn. The subdued nations are critical to the mission of the fourth beast, necessitating broader control. In *KAS*, I identified the three power-centers subdued by the

---

[90] Huxley, Aldous. *Brave New World*. London: Chatto & Windus, 1932.

little horn; These include the Vatican, Britain and the United States. The Vatican gives the little horn religious control. Britain gives the little horn financial and legal control. Finally, the United States gives the little horn military control. With these three power-centers, the little horn bullies the whole world into submission.

The citizens of the nations the little horn controls often don't realize their homelands are controlled by foreign powers and this is by design. Nations such as the United States, with a powerful and Godly charter – the Constitution and the Bill of Rights – fell prey to insidious inside forces that brought the country to her knees. The little horn proved a master of deception, causing power-centers to yield without even using an army!

The Nasty Eagle

In 2 Esdras, God gives the prophet Ezra a dream of an eagle reigning over the whole earth. The eagle in the dream offers incredible insight into the fourth beast, the legs and feet of the statue in Daniel's dream. God showed Daniel the sequence for four secular kingdoms starting with Babylon and ending with Rome in his dream. The fourth beast represents the most alarming and powerful beast in Daniel's dream – it's the one that gave him nightmares. In *KAS*, I show how the fourth beast is the fourth seal (the pale horse) in Revelation chapter 6 and how it has already fulfilled the prophecy to "destroy a fourth of the earth by war, famine, disease, and wild beasts" (Rev 6:8 MSG). God showed Ezra a highly detailed dream focused *exclusively* on the reign of the fourth beast, depicted by an eagle:

> On the second night I had a dream: I saw rising from the sea an eagle that had twelve feathered wings and three heads. I saw it spread its wings over the whole earth, and all the winds of heaven blew upon it, and the clouds were gathered around it. I saw that out of its wings there grew opposing wings, but they became little, puny wings. But its heads were at rest; the middle head was larger than the other heads, but it, too, was at rest with them. Then I saw that the eagle flew with its wings, and it reigned over the earth and over those who inhabit it. And I saw how all things under heaven were subjected to it, and no one spoke against it—not a single creature that was on the earth (2 Esdras 11:1-6 NRSV).

Note the eagle rises from the sea. The sea, a body of water, symbolized "peoples, and multitudes, and nations and tongues" (Rev 17:15 KJV). The angel also reveals to John that the waters are where the harlot of Babylon is seated. Jesus said to His disciples in Matthew 4:19, "Follow me, and I will make you fishers of men." This verse paints a picture of followers of Jesus "fishing" men out of the ungodly world. The biblical view of the sea generally represents the ungodly world and its system. This interpretation also sets the foundation in 2 Esdras where the evil eagle rises from the sea, representing the ungodly world. Recall that both Daniel and John the Revelator also describe the fourth beast coming out of the sea (Dan. 7:3, Rev 13:1). References to the sea contain a dual meaning, as Ancient Rome first began conquests of Mediterranean seaside villages, hence the description of the beast coming out of the sea.

The eagle features three heads and twelve wings. The three heads lie dormant in Ezra's dream until the end the eagle's life. Each wing represents a ruling system or kingdom that rules for a time, then loses power. The dream starts with the first king, beginning on the right. Recall that in the Hebrew language readers read right to left, so Ezra would have understood the meaning of the rightmost king ruling first in the lineup. Continuing with Ezra's dream:

> As I watched, one wing on the right side rose up, and it reigned over all the earth. And after a time its reign came to an end, and it disappeared, so that even its place was no longer visible. Then the next wing rose up and reigned, and it continued to reign a long time. While it was reigning its end came also, so that it disappeared like the first. And a voice sounded, saying to it, "Listen to me, you who have ruled the earth all this time; I announce this to you before you disappear. After you no one shall rule as long as you have ruled, not even half as long."
>
> Then the third wing raised itself up, and held the rule as the earlier ones had done, and it also disappeared. And so it went with all the wings; they wielded power one after another and

then were never seen again. I kept looking, and in due time the wings that followed also rose up on the right side, in order to rule. There were some of them that ruled, yet disappeared suddenly; and others of them rose up, but did not hold the rule.

And after this I looked and saw that the twelve wings and the two little wings had disappeared, and nothing remained on the eagle's body except the three heads that were at rest and six little wings (2 Esdras 11:12-19 NRSV).

The passage refers to the fourth beast in Daniel, which likely began during ancient Rome in the Republican Period (509-27 BC, or 482 years), followed by the Imperial Period (27 BC-476 AD, or 503 years).[91] During Rome's Republican Period, Greece held a stronghold not toppled until 146 BC. Given the later conquest of Greece during the Republican Period, one could interpret the first king's rule, the Roman Senate, as lasting only 119 years. In the passage, the first king reigns for a time and then the second king reigns for a longer time. The Lord explains this portion of the dream, "And twelve kings shall reign in it, one after another. But the second that is to reign shall hold sway for a longer time than any other one of the twelve" (2 Esdras 12:14-15). No other singular empire held power for over 500 years since Imperial Rome.

The Lord interprets in 2 Esdras 12 the voice speaking in 2 Esdras 11:15-17 for Ezra, "As for your hearing a voice that spoke, coming not from the eagle's heads but from the midst

---

[91] Randle, Aaron. "11 Roman Emperors Who Helped Mold the Ancient World." *History,* June 8, 2023. https://www.history.com/news/timeline-emperors-roman-republic

of its body, this is the interpretation: In the midst of the time of that kingdom great struggles shall arise, and it shall be in danger of falling; nevertheless it shall not fall then, but shall *regain its former power*" (2 Esdras 12:17-18). This remarkable interpretation speaks to the fall of Ancient Rome and the revival of Rome's power through not a single capital with an emperor, but through a league of like-minded nations. The "modern" Roman system achieves total control not through Roman troops, but through the financial system of private-central-banking which controls governments.

In 2 Esdras 11:7-9, the eagle instructs its wings (the kings). "Then I saw the eagle rise upon its talons, and it uttered a cry to its wings, saying, "Do not all watch at the same time; let each sleep in its own place, and watch in its turn; but let the heads be reserved for the last." This indicates that the various kings with power along the way "keep watch." The scripture speaks to the worldly nature of various empires also driven by the same lust for power and resistance to God's Word. I immediately think of the tyranny of the Holy Roman Empire and the British Empire, both guilty of fighting religious freedom or freedom of expression, even to the point of banning the translation of the Bible into the people's native tongue. Each wing kept watch by stifling Christian revival. In the next chapter of 2 Esdras, the Lord explains the fate of the eight remaining kings:

> As for your seeing eight little wings clinging to its
> wings, this is the interpretation: Eight kings shall
> arise in it whose times shall be short and their
> years swift; two of them shall perish when the

middle of its time draws near, and four shall be kept for the time when its end approaches, but two shall be kept until the end (2 Esdras 12:19-21).

The two mighty empires that are "kept until the end" refer to two mighty kingdoms that oppose the Rome-rooted system, as represented by Ezra's eagle. These two may refer to Russia and China, who are opposing the West currently, each possessing significant military might. For instance, in recent U.N. meetings both Russia and China have aligned in supporting a ceasefire in the Gaza strip. Both Russia and China are ancient kingdoms, which were brought low in the 20th century by communism. Russia ultimately rejected communism and in China, internal struggles exist which may possibly bring them out of communism as the people revolt. Both nations are leading the charge in reducing the world's dependency on the U.S. dollar. These very well could be the two "kept until the end."

Three Heads

Ezra's dream continues to a point where the three heads of the eagle awake, align together and rule the world:

...one of the heads at rest (the one that was in the middle) suddenly awoke; it was greater than the other two heads. And I saw how it allied the two heads with itself, and how the head turned with those that were with it and devoured the two little wings that were planning to reign. Moreover, this head gained control of the whole earth, and with much oppression dominated its inhabitants; it had greater power over the world than all the wings that had gone before (2 Esdras 11:29-32).

The passage indicates that the three heads of the eagle operate as an alliance, and put down any competing power. I believe the three heads represent Britain, the Vatican, and America. These three power-centers represent the financial, religious, and military control of the fourth beast, respectively. I believe the middle head, the greatest of the three, represents Britain. The little horn, the KM, controls each nation through the central-banking system. Armed with such might, the collective fourth beast attains greater power over the world than any prior ruling system, including Ancient Rome. The two heads they put down could be Russia and China, which became weakened by communism through infiltration and controlled opposition in the 20th century.

Modern World Government

Occasionally empires flex their muscles. When we think of a display of power, we typically think of a dictator watching a military parade, complete with missiles on wheels and a synchronized march of soldiers. However, these displays don't necessarily convey "power over the whole world." I believe the Covid lockdown and subsequent vaccine campaign represented a display of power like the world never saw before. Simultaneous media stories broke in February 2020, discussing a deadly new virus that could kill millions. Governments promptly began to lock down society worldwide to "stop the spread." Initially the lock-downs would last "two weeks," so we were told.

Months later the lock-downs continued in most places, with small businesses shuttered and most churches not "allowed" to meet in person or they would face fines. Curiously, the major corporations like Costco, Wal-Mart and others increased in value as small businesses suffered. Worldwide, citizens began to dig into precious savings accounts to simply get by. Children, no longer in school, began to fall behind in their learning. Mask mandates went out worldwide, and society became a zombie-land. When attempting to speak with people, one could not even tell if they were smiling! In many countries, tyrannical leaders arrested pastors or others daring to defy government mandates.

Less than a year after the Covid story broke in February 2020, governments began purchasing Covid vaccines from Pfizer, Johnson & Johnson, and Moderna and providing them free to the public. Many U.S. government agencies such as the U.S. Department of Defense required military personnel to receive the vaccine or face discharge. The rushed vaccine and government pressure to take the vaccine proved suspect. A new scientific report by *Correlation Research in the Public Interest* estimates worldwide vaccine-related deaths top 17 million in 17 different countries.[92] This number of deaths exceeds those killed in battle in World War II, the largest and

---

[92] Redshaw, Megan. "Researchers Find COVID Vaccines Causally Linked to Increased Mortality, Estimate 17 Million Deaths." *Epoch Times,* October 2, 2023. https://archive.ph/4PCBk#selection-409.0-409.98

most violent military conflict in human history.[93] The fourth beast succeeded in murdering over 1.7 billion people through wars, war-related famine, cancer and abortion in the *last 200 years alone*.[94] The more modern our society became, the more efficient the death machine of the fourth beast became.

In other displays of power, modern governments track the movements of citizens. Intelligence agencies, telecoms and big-tech form partnerships and alliances to perform warrant-less searches on citizens. Governments simply pay service providers for the data. Newer automobiles include data-tracking devices that track speed, location as well as other data.[95] Apparently electric vehicles track even more data. With the advent of cloud technology, users fell in love with a remarkable new suite of tools to help us fill out expense reports, manage HR data, and store files. Social media allows people to connect with one another in an efficient way, and consume news. However centralized-data-centers are an excellent way for big tech companies to get to know their customers and sell this data to governments and other commercial entities. Finally, our cell phones track location, sleep patterns, conversations, contacts and other information typically stored centrally. In Ancient Rome, the intelligence apparatus consisted of sentries or spies hanging out on a street corner. Now, our governments know everything about us. If you have read the various privacy policies we are regularly asked to sign when accessing phone

---

[93] "War War II." *Defense Casualty Analysis System*, Accessed January 8, 2024.
https://dcas.dmdc.osd.mil/dcas/app/conflictCasualties/ww2
[94] Thomas, *Kingdom Age of the Saints*, 72-73
[95] Burgess, Matt. "How Your New Car Tracks You." *Wired*, June 21, 2023.
https://www.wired.com/story/car-data-privacy-toyota-honda-ford/

applications or cloud platforms, you quickly realize *nothing* is private. Scripture indicates that final collaboration of the three heads "had greater power over the world than all the wings that had gone before." Modern technology-driven society represents a fulfillment of this prophecy.

The Lion Roars

The three heads of the eagle are the final controllers of the fourth beast. The three heads are controlled by a mysterious voice. Ezra said, "I looked again and saw that the voice did not come from its heads but from the middle of its body" (2 Esdras 11:10). The voice in the middle of its body controls and gives instructions not only to the wings (rulers) as we read earlier, but also to the three heads remaining at the end. Clearly this voice represents a satanic voice. The little horn, guided by Satan, directs the fourth beast. I believe the fourth seal in Revelation chapter 6 provides further insight into the fourth beast. Revelation 6:8 (MSG) describes him as "A colorless horse, sickly pale. Its rider was Death, and Hell was close on its heels. They were given power to destroy a fourth of the earth by war, famine, disease, and wild beasts." In Daniel 11:39, scripture indicates the little horn is helped by a "foreign god." Guided by Satan, the little horn tells the heads what to do until the Lion of the Tribe of Judah shuts him down.

My family greatly enjoys C.S. Lewis' *The Chronicles of Narnia* book series.[96] The novels gloriously tell the story of Jesus through a series of brilliantly-written fantasy-books for

---

[96] Lewis, C.S. *Chronicles of Narnia*. London: Geoffrey Bles, The Bodley Head, HarperCollins, 1950-1956.

children. In *The Chronicles of Narnia,* the key character is a lion named Aslan. In *The Lion, the Witch and the Wardrobe,* the first book published in the series, Aslan willingly sacrifices himself to save a "son of Adam," before rising from the dead and defeating the evil white witch.[97] Aslan, the lion in C.S. Lewis' series represents Jesus, who sacrificed Himself for mankind and then rose from the dead to save humanity as our Savior. In Revelation 5:5 (NRSV), the apostle John writes "see, the Lion of the tribe of Judah, the Root of David, has conquered." We see the lion of the tribe of Judah in action in the book of 2 Esdras, when a lion roused from the forest delivers to the evil eagle a compelling statement of judgment from God:

> Hear thou, I will talk with thee, and the Highest shall say unto thee, Art not thou it that remainest of the four beasts, whom I made to reign in my world, that the end of their times might come through them? And the fourth came, and overcame all the beasts that were past, and had power over the world with great fearfulness, and over the whole compass of the earth with much wicked oppression; and so long time dwelt he upon the earth with deceit.
>
> For the earth hast thou not judged with truth. For thou hast afflicted the meek, thou hast hurt the peaceable, thou hast loved liars, and destroyed the dwellings of them that brought

---

[97]   Lewis, C.S. *The Lion, the Witch and the Wardrobe.* London: Geoffrey Bles, HarperCollins, 1950.

forth fruit, and hast cast down the walls of such as did thee no harm. Therefore is thy wrongful dealing come up unto the Highest, and thy pride unto the Mighty. The Highest also hath looked upon the proud times, and behold, they are ended, and his abominations are fulfilled.

And therefore appear no more, thou eagle, nor thy horrible wings, nor thy wicked feathers, nor thy malicious heads, nor thy hurtful claws, nor all thy vain body: that all the earth may be refreshed, and may return, being delivered from thy violence, and that she may hope for the judgment and mercy of him that made her (2 Esdras 11:38-46 KJV).

The lion calls out the vicious fourth beast and points out the tyranny associated with his reign. He mentions that the fourth beast rules with fear and wicked oppression of the innocent. The lion also points out the fourth beast loves liars. I have worked with a couple of evil people before and notice evil leaders somehow prefer working with other evil people – "birds of a feather flock together." Note the lion calls out the fourth beast for destroying the dwellings of them that brought forth fruit. When Jesus refers to His servants that bear fruit, He is talking about those who live with Christian character who are effective at bringing Christ's message to the world. The fourth beast vehemently hates Christians.

Just before Jesus judges the fourth beast, He says "his [God's] abominations are fulfilled." When God delivers judgment on an empire, He waits until the level of hateful acts and unrepentant pride reaches a tipping point worthy of judgment to deliver His children in a mighty way. For instance, when God spoke to Abraham about how his descendants would suffer under slavery in Egypt, He discusses His forthcoming judgment. God told Abraham, "after four generations your descendants will return here to this land [the promised land], for the sins of the Amorites do not yet warrant their destruction" (Gen. 15:16 NLT). God planned to judge Egypt in a big way, transferring all their wealth to His children. He also planned to give other land to Israel. When Egypt began killing the male children among Israel to "thin the herd," God began to speak to Moses and relay His redemptive plan now that the sins of the Egyptians warranted the destruction of Egypt. Abortion programs in the last 100 years killed *1 billion* babies, worldwide. The sins of the fourth beast call out for an extreme judgment – we've reached God's judgment tipping point.

Note near the end of the passage in 2 Esdras, God judges the fourth beast with ease. No battle – just the pronouncement that the fourth beast "appear no more." I love this passage. It indicates the power of God over our enemy, Satan. One day, the Lord says "no more" to Satan's gigantic, bloated apparatus and soon thereafter, the government of the land shifts to God's people. There is more to it, because the Soldier Saints assume a role in judging the fourth beast and bring his minions to justice. My point is that God does not need to fight with Satan to defeat him – He simply speaks the Word, and it is so.

The Kingdom Age of the Saints

In *KAS*, I discuss how God plans to give the geopolitical dominion of the world to the saints after He judges the fourth beast. Jesus gave Christians spiritual authority when He defeated death, hell and the grave after rising from the dead. Jesus commanded His disciples to heal the sick, cast out devils, and raise the dead (Matt. 10:8). However, Jesus refused to address Rome's governmental authority. Jesus did not come to topple Rome during His earthly ministry – that would happen later. I imagine Jesus knew that Rome's sins did not *yet* warrant destruction. I also believe Jesus studied the prophetic dreams and visions of Daniel and Ezra and knew Rome's lease on governing the world geopolitically would extend for a couple of thousand more years. Understanding God's ways helps us understand His statement to the fourth beast, "Art not thou it that remainest of the four beasts, whom I made to reign in my world, that the end of their [the beasts] times might come through them?" (2 Esdras 11:38 KJV). God permitted the fourth beast – the most evil of the beasts – to usher in the end of their (the beasts) times. The end of the fourth and final beast ends the times of the Gentiles which Jesus spoke of in Luke 21:24.

The judgment of the fourth beast also ushers in a wealth transfer and conveyance of power in the Kingdom Age of the Saints – much like what God did for Israel. God promises a refreshing for *all the earth*. 2 Esdras 11:46 (KJV), says, "That all the earth may be refreshed, and may return, being delivered from thy violence, and that she may hope for the judgment and mercy of him that made her." We garner further insight related to this passage, as God further interprets the passage for Ezra in 2 Esdras 12:34. "For the rest of my people shall he deliver with mercy, those that have been pressed upon my borders, and he shall make them joyful until the coming of the day of judgment, whereof I have spoken unto thee from the beginning." Wow, these are amazing promises!

First, all the earth is refreshed – not just people, God's prized creation. It also includes the animals, the sea, the sky and the land. The Hebrew word for "refreshed" is the same word used in Exodus 31:17, "It is a sign between me and the children of Israel for ever: for in six days the Lord made heaven and earth, and on the seventh day he rested, and was refreshed." God rested on the seventh day, not from fatigue. He rested on the seventh day to *enjoy His creation.* The refreshing coming for the whole earth allows all creation to enjoy the earth and each other. I am reminded of Romans 8:21 (NLT), "the creation looks forward to the day when it will join God's children in glorious freedom from death and decay."

The passage in 2 Esdras 12:34 says God makes His people "joyful until the coming of the day of judgment." This passage indicates that, after the fourth beast is judged, God's people experience joy all the way until a *day of judgment.* Note this verse refers to the time *after* God judges the fourth beast. But which day of judgment does this scripture reference? The scripture refers to the Great White Throne Judgment in Revelation 20:11-15. In *KAS*, I state that God's people are raptured from the Kingdom Age of the Saints *into* the Marriage Supper of the Lamb. We don't endure the judgment of evil people during the time of the Great Tribulation, a time when Satan rules the world in a short, last hurrah. Instead, we simply walk into Heaven and enjoy a multi-year celebration and ceremony when Jesus "marries" His Bride. Isn't God's plan wonderful! Glory to God!

According to 2 Esdras 11:46, creation joins God's children in a time of glorious freedom after the fourth beast is judged. The passage mentions that earth "returns." Returns to what? God's people return to the very place everything started for mankind. The place where man lived in a land that supported him and fed him without sweat or labor. We return to a type of the Garden of Eden.

Return to the Garden

The Garden of Eden represented a type of paradise. Adam and Eve enjoyed intimate fellowship with God. They did not toil in the garden – they rested and enjoyed God's beautiful creation. The Garden of Eden did not represent Heaven, for Satan gained access to tempt man in the Garden. When we arrive in Heaven, Satan is not there. In Eden, "God blessed them, and God said unto them, 'Be fruitful, and multiply, and replenish the earth, and subdue it: and have dominion over the fish of the sea, and over the fowl of the air, and over every living thing that moveth upon the earth'" (Gen. 1:28 KJV). This command required man to subdue the earth, meaning to bring it under control. In Genesis 2:15, God put man in the Garden to dress it and to keep it. Both of these verses indicate that man needed to protect the Garden and take care of it.

Inside the Garden of Eden stood the Tree of Life. When God drove man from the garden after he yielded to the serpent, God "placed at the east of the garden of Eden Cherubims, and a flaming sword which turned every way, to keep the way of the tree of life" (Gen. 3:24). Note the Cherubims guarded the Tree of Life, which according to Genesis 3:22, produces the fruit of longevity.

In *KAS*, God revealed to me a riddle in the book of Revelation that provides a detailed description of promises related to the Kingdom Age of the Saints. The very first promise in the riddle is Revelation 2:7 (CEV), "I will let everyone who wins the victory eat from the life-giving tree in God's wonderful garden." In *KAS*, I show that saints in the Kingdom Age experience a much longer lifespan than in the current age, but now I see there is more to it. Combining Revelation 2:7 with the promise of 2 Esdras 11:46, it appears that during the Kingdom Age of the Saints, we return to a time much like Adam and Eve experienced in the Garden of Eden! The earth produced for them without sweat and toil – with their every need met. In the Garden of Eden, resources abounded. Most importantly, man enjoyed unique fellowship with God in the Garden. It said that God walked in the Garden in the cool of the day (Gen. 3:8). In the Kingdom Age, God's glory fills the earth, a yet unfulfilled promise to His people (Num. 14:21, Hab. 2:14, Isa. 11:9, Rev 18:1). We also experience glorious fellowship with God on a new level.

8. Death of the Three-Headed Eagle

The eagle that you saw coming up from the sea is the fourth kingdom that appeared in a vision to your brother Daniel.

– 2 Esdras 12:11 NRSV

The Bible is amazing. Thousands of years ago, God wrote the future through His prophets. Recall the story of King Cyrus. Over one hundred years before King Cyrus' birth, God mentions him by name in Isaiah chapters 44-45 and in other parts of the Bible. God spoke about Cyrus long *before* Israel went into captivity in Babylon and called King Cyrus to deliver them before his birth! King Cyrus discovered himself in the Word of God to know what he needed to do to defeat Babylon. He also discovered himself in Jeremiah's scrolls, and knew to let Israel rebuild God's temple, fulfilling written Bible prophecy. This story proves that God plans the future of humanity in advance. It should not be a surprise to us that same level of detail exists for the demise of the fourth beast system, the most evil beast.

Before Israel went into Egyptian slavery, God warned their patriarch, Abram. God always tells His prophets the future. He told Abram:

> Abram, you will live to an old age and die in peace. But I solemnly promise that your descendants will live as foreigners in a land that doesn't belong to them. They will be forced into slavery and abused for four hundred years. But I will terribly punish the nation that enslaves them, and they will leave with many possessions. Four generations later, your descendants will return here and take this land, because only then will the people who live here be so sinful that they deserve to be punished (Gen. 15:12b-16 CEV).

So here we are, thousands of years later, living under the debt slavery system of the fourth beast. As He did with Abram, God gives us specific promises about how our redemption occurs. The fourth beast in 2 Esdras represents the current, Rome-rooted fourth beast system. The eagle's three heads represent the final power-centers ruling the fourth beast. The three heads listen to a voice guiding them, the voice of the little horn depicted in Daniel's vision (the KM), which by extension is the voice of Satan. How the three-headed eagle dies in 2 Esdras provides amazing clues as to how God executes His judgment and sets mankind free from the grip of the fourth beast.

Story of the Eagle

Initially, Ezra failed to understand the dream God gave him. God in His mercy interpreted the dream for Ezra. For instance, in 2 Esdras 11, God gave Ezra the complete dream, but in the next chapter (2 Esdras 12), He interpreted many parts of the dream for Ezra. In the dream, we learn about the final days of the eagle before its downfall:

> Moreover, this head gained control of the whole earth, and with much oppression dominated its inhabitants; it had greater power over the world than all the wings that had gone before.
>
> After this I looked again and saw the head in the middle suddenly disappear, just as the wings had done. But the two heads remained, which also in like manner ruled over the earth and its inhabitants. And while I looked, I saw the head on the right side devour the one on the left (2 Esdras 11:32-35 NRSV).

In this passage, we learn that the middle head disappears suddenly. Then the remaining two heads continue on as if nothing happened. Finally, the second head is devoured by the third. Readers may ask, what does this mean? Thankfully, the Lord interprets this portion of the dream:

And whereas thou sawest that the great head appeared no more, it signifieth that one of them shall die upon his bed, and yet with pain. For the two that remain shall be slain with the sword. For the sword of the one shall devour the other: but at the last shall he fall through the sword himself (2 Esdras 12:26-28 KJV).

The passage indicates a final scenario where all three heads are slain. The last part of the passage gives incredible clues for humanity's future. When the Lord showed me the meaning of the passage, it gave me hope for America.

Middle Head Dies in Bed and Disappears

I believe the middle head of the statue represents Britain, and more specifically, the City of London Corporation. Rome conquered the British Isles beginning in AD 43 under Emperor Claudius.[98] Julius Caesar later invaded Britain and forced the British warlord Cassivellaunus to surrender. Britain produced a great deal of tin and proved an ideal merchant-marine trading-post. The law and practice of the Romans, the founders of the City of London, became the basis of London's institutions and political language. In the Magna Carta, the AD 1215 Charter of Rights between King John and the barons, it was agreed that the City of London be separate from the Crown.[99] In 1632, the Crown asked the Corporation

---

[98]   Wikipedia. 2024. "Roman Conquest of Britain." Wikimedia Foundation. Last modified February 5, 2024. https://en.wikipedia.org/wiki/Roman_conquest_of_Britain.

[99]   Glasman, Maurice. "The City of London's strange history: Lord Glasman on what the Romans did for the Square Mile" *Financial Times,* September 29, 2014. https://www.ft.com/content/7c8f24fa-3aa5-11e4-bd08-00144feabdc0

to extend privileges to additional populus within the City of London, but the Corporation refused and instead transferred unwanted, excess population elsewhere by 1637, dubbed the "great refusal" (of the Crown). The Corporation of London clearly established precedent over the Crown.

Any efforts by the Crown to change the arrangement with the Corporation were met with violence indicative of KM control. The Bishops' Wars (1639-40) and the English Civil War (1642-51) agitated conflict between the reigning British monarchy and Parliament, and Parliament won the battle. A final effort by Charles II to establish the Stuart monarchy as the source of the Corporation's authority led to his replacement by William and Mary, whose Second Charter in 1690 firmly cemented the City of London as a sovereign city-state.

During the 18th century, the City of London backed George Washington *against the Crown*, providing funds and men for the cause of the U.S. Republic. The citizens of London reminded the king, to the point of treason, that it was *they* and not he who won the civil war in Britain. The KM recognized that headstrong monarchs were a threat to the more easily influenced Parliament model of governance. When the "banking class" was challenged by a monarchy, agitating civil war and unrest appeared to be the weapon of choice to bring those monarchies into subjection.

The Rome-rooted City of London held considerable sway over the governance of Britain, and used its influence to cast Britain into war whenever commercially expedient. Early wars by Britain largely supported the slave trade as well as the aggregation of natural resources. By the early 1600s, Britain began to conquer lands all across the world. Figure 2 shows the British conquests which built up the British Empire. Figure 2 lists *over 100* conquests, possession or settlements by the British Empire of formerly sovereign territories between 1600 and 1930.

By the turn of the 20th century, The British Empire produced one-third of the coal supply of the world, one-sixth of the wheat supply and two-thirds of the gold supply. Trading companies founded most of the American and West Indian colonies. A trading company won India and a trading company colonized the northwestern districts of Canada. Commercial wars during the greater part of the 18th century established the British command of the seas. These same wars gave Britain South Africa and chartered companies in the 19th century carried the British flag into the interior of the African continent from the south, east, and west. At home, in the latter half of the 17th century and the earlier part of the 18th century, parliamentary power had taken the place of the divine right of kings. In Great Britain, customs duties from trade accounted for about half the national income. At the turn of the 20th century, throughout the empire and notably in the United Kingdom, a considerable presence of Jewish blood existed among the white races.[100]

---

[100] Lugard, Sir F. "British Empire." *The Encyclopaedia Britannica*, 11th ed. 4:607.

Figure 2: Conquests of the British Empire[101]

Year Range	Conquest, Possession, or Settlement
1600 to 1650	Barbados, Bermudas, Gambia, St. Christopher, Novia Scotia, Nevis, Montserrat, Antigua, Honduras, St. Lucia, Gold Coast, Bombay
1651 to 1700	St. Helena, Jamaica, Bahamas, Virgin Islands, N.W. Territories of Canada, Turks and Caicos Islands, Madras, Bengal
1701 to 1750	Gibraltar, New Brunswick
1751 to 1800	Ontario, Quebec, Dominica, St. Vincent, Grenada, Tobago, Falkan Islands, Saskatchewan, Pitcairn Islands, Straits Settlements, Sierra Leone, Alberta, New South Wales, Ceylon, Trinidad, Malta, United Provinces of Agra and Oudh
1801 to 1850	British Guiana, Tasmania, Cape of Good Hope, Seycheles, Mauritius, Manitoba, Ascension and Tristan da Cunha, British Columbia and Vancouver Island, Natal, Queensland, West Australia, Victoria, South Australia, New Zealand, Hong-Kong, Labuan, Central Indian Provinces, Eastern Bengal and Assam, Burma, Punjab, Ajmere and Merwara, Coorg
1851 to 1900	Lagos, Basutoland, Fiji, West Pacific Islands, Foderated Malay States, Cyprus, North Borneo, Papua, Nigeria, Somaliland, Bechuanaland, Zululand, Sarawak, Brunei, British East Africa, Rhodesia, Zanzibar, Uganda, Nyasaland, Ashanti, Wei-hai-wei, Pacific Islands, Orange Free State, Transvaal and Swaziland, British Baluchistan, Andaman Islands
1901 to 1930	Kelantan, Trengganu, N.W. Frontier Indian Province, Palestine, Transjordan, Iraq, Cameroon, Togoland, Tanganyika, South Africa, Egypt

[101] Lugard, Sir F, "British Empire." *The Encyclopaedia Britannica, 11th ed.* (Cambridge, UK: Cambridge University Press, 1911), 4:606-613. Wikipedia. 2024. "British Empire." Wikimedia Foundation. Last modified February 11, 2024. https://en.wikipedia.org/wiki/British_Empire

Queen Elizabeth II reigned as queen of the United Kingdom for over 70 years, the longest reign of any British monarch.[102] The queen, however, likely possessed little power compared with the controllers of the City of London. Queen Elizabeth needed to seek permission to visit the City of London from its Lord Mayor.[103] However, to the public, the queen represented the United Kingdom. When Queen Elizabeth died on September 8, 2022, an era ended. President Trump met with Queen Elizabeth in July 2018 and onlookers noted he walked in front of the queen, a break of strict protocol.

Many suspect that President Trump negotiated America out of a treaty dating back to 1871 involving the United Kingdom and the Vatican that had eroded United States' sovereignty. I believe the death of the Queen fulfilled the prophecy in 2 Esdras 12:26, that one of the three heads would die in their bed. Soon, I hope we will discover all the details regarding the City of London and the British Crown in relation to the biblical prophecy.

The Third Devours the Second

The second head of the eagle suffers at the hand of the third. I believe the second head of the eagle represents the Vatican, devoured by the third head of the eagle, the United States.

The Vatican represents the headquarters of the Catholic Church. The Catholic Church owns property across the world spanning nearly 300 thousand square miles, about the size of

[102] Wikipedia. 2024. "Elizabeth II." Wikimedia Foundation. Last modified February 7, 2024. https://en.wikipedia.org/wiki/Elizabeth_II.
[103] "8 Quizzical Queen Facts." *The London Bicycle Tour Company.* *https://www.londonbicycle.com/blog/8-quizzical-queen-facts*

the state of Texas.[104] It is estimated that the Vatican's real estate holdings top $220 billion in 2024 dollars.[105] The Catholic Church controls a priceless trove of art, contained in 54 museums including the Sistine Chapel. Works include art pieces by Raphael, Michelangelo, and Vincent Van Gogh.[106] "Father" Richard Ginder, the American editor of the Catholic Weekly, wrote in a 1963 column:

> The Catholic Church must be the biggest corporation in the United States. We have a branch office in almost every neighborhood. Our assets and real estate holdings must exceed those of Standard Oil, AT&T and U.S. Steel combined. And our roster of dues-paying members be second only to the tax rolls of the United States government.[107]

Like many other leaders in the Catholic Church, Ginder was arrested for possession of child pornography and sentenced to ten years probation. He later published a book in 1976 critical of the church's doctrines on sexuality which led to his eviction from the priesthood. In 1978, he was arrested, tried and convicted of sodomizing two underage boys and

[104] Jacobs, Frank. "What do King Charles III, the Pope, and Canadian Inuit have in common?" *Big Think,* June 16, 2023. https://bigthink.com/strange-maps/worlds-largest-landowners/

[105] Bello, Nino Lo. *The Vatican Empire.* (Trident Press, 1969). 96-97

[106] Runo, Kennedy. "10 Interesting Facts About Vatican Museum." *Jubilee Travel,* Accessed January 21, 2024. https://www.jubileeonline.ca/10-interesting-facts-about-vatican-museum#:~:text=The%20Vatican%20Museums%20were%20founded,della%20Segnatura%20decorated%20by%20Raphael.

[107] Gollin, James. *Worldly Goods: The Wealth and Power of the American Catholic Church, the Vatican, and the Men Who Control the Money.* (NY: Random House, 1971). 6.

sentenced to four years in prison.[108] The New York Times reported *in Pennsylvania alone*, more than 300 priests were found to have abused at least 1,000 children over the course of seven decades.[109]

In many circles, rumors circulated about vast troves of gold held in custody by the Catholic Church in tunnels underneath the Vatican. In an August 2023 interview on *GB News*, Dr. Jan Halper-Hayes indicated the U.S. military previously raided the Vatican and removed "650 planes" full of gold.[110] Dr. Halper-Hayes claimed she sits on a task force for the U.S. military. She referenced a video in which President Trump met with Pope Francis, who looked extremely unhappy.[111] She also pointed out that President Trump walked in front of Queen Elizabeth II during his visit on July 14, 2018 and renegotiated an 1871 treaty.[112] Her claim that the U.S. raided the Vatican gold was reinforced by many others on social media making similar claims.

In an unprecedented move, on August 23, 2022, Pope Frances ordered all connected entities to move all financial assets to the Vatican Bank within 30 days of September 1,

[108] "5 Pittsburgh Priests Went to Prison," *Pittsburg Post-Gazette,* February 28, 2004. https://www.post-gazette.com/news/nation/2004/02/28/5-Pittsburgh-priests-went-to-prison/stories/200402280131

[109] Graham, Ruth. "What the Latest Investigations Into Catholic Church Sex Abuse Mean." *The New York Times,* June 2, 2023. https://www.nytimes.com/2023/06/02/us/catholic-church-sex-abuse-investigations.html#:~:text=More%20than%20300%20priests%20were,and%20sorrow%E2%80%9D%20over%20the%20findings.

[110] "Stephen Dixon Clashes with Guest on Trump Claims of Rigged Election: 'He Knows It Wasn't'." Youtube.Com/@GBNewsOnline. August 3, 2023. Video, https://www.youtube.com/watch?v=l0WacP1CrWY.

[111] "President Trump Meets Pope Francis (C-SPAN)." Youtube.Com/@CSPAN. May 24, 2017. Video, https://www.youtube.com/watch?v=-kgQ7bBxMt4.

[112] "Trump Breaks Royal Etiquette, Walks in Front of Queen." Youtube.Com/@Globalnews. July 14, 2018. Video, https://www.youtube.com/watch?v=tyBKS-rV4eE.

2022.[113] The Vatican Bank "margin call" indicates a form of financial panic hitting the Vatican Bank. If the Vatican Bank's assets were earlier seized by the U.S. military, then perhaps this would explain any financial shortfall.

If in fact the U.S. military did seize the Vatican's assets, that act would fulfill Ezra's prophecy that the sword of the third head devours the second head of the eagle in 2 Esdras 12:26-28. Of course, pundits immediately ask, "What would be the legal basis of the U.S. military seizing the assets of the Vatican?" On December 21, 2017, President Trump issued an executive order entitled, "Executive Order Blocking the Property of Persons Involved in Serious Human Rights Abuse or Corruption."[114] In the order, President Trump maintained the right to seize the assets of any foreign person or entity "to be responsible for or complicit in, or to have directly or indirectly engaged in, serious human rights abuse." President Trump issued a handful of such executive orders as president and many wondered how, when or if the orders would be carried out. This executive order would have given President Trump or the military, acting on his behalf, the legal right to seize the Vatican's assets.

The Third Falls on His Own Sword

The third head of the eagle falls on its own sword but does not disappear as did the middle head (Britain). 2 Esdras

---

[113] Brockhaus, Hannah. "Pope Francis instructs Vatican entities to move all funds to Vatican bank by Sept. 30." *Catholic News Agency,* August 23, 2022. https://www.catholicnewsagency.com/news/252093/pope-francis-instructs-vatican-entities-to-move-all-funds-to-vatican-bank-by-sept-30

[114] "Executive Order Blocking the Property of Persons Involved in Serious Human Rights Abuse or Corruption." *White House Archives,* December 21, 2017. "https://trumpwhitehouse.archives.gov/presidential-actions/executive-order-blocking-property-persons-involved-serious-human-rights-abuse-corruption/

12:28 mentions, "the last shall he fall through the sword himself" (KJV). I believe the last head discussed in the verse represents the United States, and more specifically the United States Corporation. The U.S. military served the little horn well over the last 110 years. We fought banker's battles, enriching the little horn and cementing control over nations through the subsequent installation of private-central-banks in conquered nations. The bankers sent America's treasure – young men and women in the prime of their lives – to war to enrich the corporate-elite. Almost every war started out with the oft-used propaganda slogan, "If we fight the war there, it won't come here." We typically discovered later that the original reason for attacking other countries was based on a lie. For instance, President Bush ordered the attack on Iraq in March 2003 based on the presence of purported weapons of mass destruction (WMDs). The WMDs were never found. President Bush later joked with the press corps about the search for WMDs.[115] In my view, Bush's humor revealed the deep-rooted elitist attitude of nobility vs. the peasants – send the peasants to war while the elites divide the spoils. The winners of the Iraq war were the government contractors, including Halliburton.

Many members of the U.S. military suffer a secondary type of Post Traumatic Stress Syndrome (PTSD) after serving in Iraq and other wars; They realize the wars they bravely fought benefited the bankers, not the American people. Many paid the ultimate price. American military members

---

[115] Teather, David. "Bush jokes about search for WMD, but it's no laughing matter for critics." *The Guardian*, March 26, 2004.
https://www.theguardian.com/world/2004/mar/26/usa.iraq

suffer "battle PTSD" from direct battlefield warfare and also "emotional PTSD" from being lied to by their government. Decades of bankers' wars and an awakening among military families produced a split in the military. Today, there are U.S. service members still loyal to President Trump, who stayed out of war during his first term. Other service members are loyal to Biden, who threatened to send U.S. troops to Ukraine to fight Russia if Congress failed to approve funding.[116] The split of allegiance within the ranks of the U.S. military provides the backdrop for Ezra's dream. Somehow, someway the U.S. military *removes its own head.*

The Lord told Ezra the third head falls on its own sword. The sword is the U.S. military. The U.S. military removes the interloper, usurper head of the United States, the KM. In a *stunning* prophecy delivered approximate*ly* 2,500 years ago, God told us what happens next for America. Americans recognize our three civilian branches of government are compromised and no longer function as intended. The judicial branch represents a two-tiered justice system protecting elites at the expense of patriots. The legislative branch marches forward to advance the uni-party spending plans, further indebting our children and grandchildren. The executive branch became occupied by a man who ran his campaign from his basement on *zoom* calls. Biden literally bragged about election fraud before the 2020 election (see Chapter 6). The civilian safeguards designed to protect the United States from foreign power are broken. I

---

[116] Milligan, Susan. "Biden: Help Ukraine Now or Send Americans to Fight Russia With NATO Later." *US News,* December 6, 2023. https://www.usnews.com/news/national-news/articles/2023-12-06/biden-help-ukraine-now-or-send-americans-to-fight-russia-with-nato-later

believe the military is the only way to fix the problem. According to the prophet Ezra, the U.S. military delivers America from foreign powers.

Two Horns of the anti-Christ

In Revelation 13:1 (NLT), John describes his vision of the fourth beast. "Then I saw a *beast* rising up out of the sea. It had seven heads and ten horns, with ten crowns on its horns. And written on each head were names that blasphemed God." Given the reference to ten horns and seven heads, we recognize this as the fourth beast, coming out of the sea. A few verses later, we read about the beast *after* the fourth beast, the *fifth* beast. In Revelation 13:11-12, we read:

> Then I saw *another* beast come up out of the earth. He had two horns like those of a lamb, but he spoke with the voice of a dragon. He exercised all the authority of the first beast. And he required all the earth and its people to worship the first beast, whose fatal wound had been healed.

The fifth beast represents the dragon (the anti-Christ) who rules for a short time during the Great Tribulation. In Revelation 13:11, the fifth beast has "two horns" and comes out of the earth rather than the sea.

In 2 Esdras we learn how the three heads of the eagle die. However, God also provides clues about the fifth beast. In 2 Esdras 12:29-30, God shows us how two horns carry over into another era:

As for your seeing two little wings passing over to the head which was on the right side, this is the interpretation: It is these whom the Most High has kept for the eagle's end; this was the reign which was brief and full of tumult, as you have seen.

Two heads present in the reign of the fourth beast end up arising and leading during the time of the anti-Christ. The anti-Christ exercises all the authority of the fourth beast. He reigns over the earth and implements great tyranny. For instance, while the fourth beast kills about 25 percent of humanity (already fulfilled), an additional one-third of humanity dies during the time of the anti-Christ. The anti-Christ subdues two powerful nations that exist today to execute his control in the latter days, during the Great Tribulation. Right now I can't predict which two nations the anti-Christ subdues to execute his bidding in the Great Tribulation, although China remains a possibility. I am sure 250 years ago, no one could predict that the United States would become such a great contributor to the efforts of the fourth beast. Founded by strong Christians with a noble vision, we fell to the little horn in 1913 (or even as early as 1871).

Time will tell which two nations become the foundational nations used by the anti-Christ in the last day to establish rule. To be clear, I don't think we should consume a lot of time thinking about it. As Christians, we "majored on the minor" for many decades by remaining hyper-focused on the anti-Christ hundreds of years before he will appear. This cycle of fear-mongering by even Church leaders kept Christians in bondage. According to God's timetable, the Church will be celebrating in Heaven at the Marriage Supper of the Lamb during the Great Tribulation. Armed with the glory of God and powerful evangelical outreach during the Kingdom Age, we bring *billions* of people to Jesus. Any person that rejects God during the Kingdom Age, after being exposed to the glorious generosity and mercies of God, will suffer under the anti-Christ during the Great Tribulation. God's mercies are great, and even those that remain in the Great Tribulation may access the 144,000 member evangelical team reserved for them (Rev 7:4).

9. Age of Days

The age has lost its youth, and the times begin to grow old...

– 2 Esdras 14:10 NRSV

When God gave me the revelation to write *KAS*, I underestimated the significance of the title. Only after making new discoveries in 2 Esdras, did I realize that the Kingdom Age of the Saints marks the beginning of a *brand new age*. I then found many English Bible translations mistranslate or use interchangeably "age" and "world." For instance, many translations represent the disciples' question to Jesus in Matthew 24:3 as, "Tell us ... of the end of the world" (KJV)? Yet Jesus went on to describe the end of the age, not the end of the world. The translation matters. Many immediately think of their favorite apocalyptic film when they hear the phrase "end of the world." When we think of the "end of the world," we typically associate the phrase with the destruction of earth. For all recorded history, mankind lived in the same age on the same earth.

However, what God reveals to Ezra represents a game-changer. Turns out the age we are in ends soon and a new one begins. I feel in my heart God chose us for this generation for a special reason. If you are reading this book, God handpicked *you* to experience a transition to an entirely new age. The Kingdom Age of the Saints represents the first chapter in a brand new age. There are some clues in the New Testament about a new age. For instance in Hebrews we read:

> For it is impossible, in the case of those who have once been enlightened, who have tasted the heavenly gift, and have shared in the Holy Spirit, and have tasted the goodness of the word of God and the *powers of the age to come*, and then have fallen away, to restore them again to repentance, since they are crucifying once again the Son of God to their own harm and holding him up to contempt (Heb. 6:4-6 ESV, emphasis added).

This passage describes how a Believer that denies God after experiencing all God offers endangers his or her salvation. Note it says Believers who have tasted the "powers of the age to come." Which age is the writer referring to? And what are the powers of the next age? Clearly, the passage refers to an age *after* the present age.

12 Days of the Age

Moses possessed a special relationship with God. He communed on Mount Sinai with God for days (Ex. 24:18). God even showed Moses His glory (Ex. 34:5-8). God tells Ezra about His relationship with Moses:

> ...I led him up on Mount Sinai, where I kept him with me many days. I told him many wondrous things, and showed him the secrets of the times and declared to him the end of the times. Then I commanded him, saying, 'These words you shall publish openly, and these you shall keep secret' (2 Esdras 14:4-5 NRSV).

In this remarkable passage, God reveals the intimacy of His relationship with Moses. I believe He desires the same level of intimacy with us today. We find out that during Moses' time on Mount Sinai, God shared with him the "secrets of the times" as well as "the end of the times." The secrets God shared with Moses may be why no one knows where Moses was buried – he may have simply been taken into Heaven like Enoch, armed with new knowledge about how to transcend time into a place without time. I believe God showed Moses the end of the times, or the same vision he showed Daniel, Ezra and John the Revelator. All these prophets wrote down the same story – however, varying in detail.

The story of Moses on Mount Sinai instructs us on the sinful nature of mankind and why some are special to God. Moses *wanted* to be with God in the cloud of glory, while the people did not. In Exodus 20:18-19, we learn "All the people, experiencing the thunder and lightning, the trumpet blast and the smoking mountain, were afraid - they pulled back and *stood at a distance.* They said to Moses, 'You speak to us and we'll listen, but don't have God speak to us or we'll die'" (MSG emphasis added). The people stood at a distance, even though God gave them permission to come closer. Today, many religious doctrines separate us from God and block the secrets He desires to share with us. To learn God's secrets, we must draw near to Him.

God shares a massively important revelation with Ezra regarding the days of the age in 2 Esdras 14:

> The age has lost its youth, and the times begin to grow old. For the age is divided into twelve parts, and nine of its parts have already passed, as well as half of the tenth part; so two of its parts remain, besides half of the tenth part (vv. 10-12 NRSV).
>
> For evils worse than those that you have now seen happen shall take place hereafter. For the weaker the world becomes through old age, the more shall evils be increased upon its inhabitants. Truth shall go farther away, and falsehood shall come near. For the eagle that you saw in the vision is already hurrying to come (vv. 16-18).

Here we learn that the age Ezra lived in begins to grow old. We find that as the world gets older, more evils increase upon humanity. The Bible indicates many falsehoods "come near," or said another way, become broadly accepted. God shares with Ezra that He divided the present age into 12 parts. I believe these "parts" represent *days* of the age of the length of 1,000 years. In 2 Peter 3:8, we learn that "with the Lord one day is like a thousand years, and a thousand years are like one day." I interpret each part of the age as a day lasting 1,000 years. In Figure 3, we see the "days of the age" with an overlay of important biblical and geopolitical events during each 1,000 year "day" of the age. The present age ends with the Stone Judgment, prophesied in Daniel 2 and synonymous with the sixth seal in Revelation 6.

I call days one-through-six the "undiscovered days." The Bible records very little about what happened. They could be the six days of creation in Genesis. Of major significance are God's words to Ezra when He says, "so two of its parts remain, besides half of the tenth part." If one interprets the parts of the age as 1,000 year segments, then according to God, only 2,500 years remained in the age when He gave Ezra the dream. But when did God give Ezra the dream? According to biblical scholars, Ezra led a group of exiled Judeans back to Jerusalem in 458 BC.[117] Other scholars point out that Ezra moved into the prophetic and describes his own genealogy in Ezra 7:1 (KJV). Here Ezra writes, "Now after these things," referring to the interval between the sixth

---

[117]   Remmers, Arend. "Book Overview – Ezra." *StudyLight,* Accessed January 10, 2024. https://www.studylight.org/commentaries/eng/bcc/ezra.html

year of Darius (BC 516) and the seventh of Artaxerxes (BC 458), dating Ezra between these two time frames.[118]

We don't know precisely when Ezra wrote 2 Esdras. But using a range of the two dates and adding 2,500 years takes us to between AD 1984 and AD 2042. However, it appears Ezra wrote 2 Esdras near the *end* of his lifetime, for God tells him, "for you shall be taken up from among humankind, and henceforth you shall live with my Son and with those who are like you, until the times are ended" (2 Esdras 14:9 NRSV). We know mankind did not move into the Kingdom Age in AD 1984, however, according to the timeline God gave Ezra, the "old" age will be ending soon!

In my book *KAS* I indicate I believe God told Daniel the fourth beast would rule the world geopolitically for 2,150 years. This is based on my interpretation of the prophecy that the fourth beast would be given authority for "a time, two times, and half a time" in the Bible (Dan. 7:25, 12:7). To explain, "times" equals 1,000 years (two times equals 2,000 years), while "time" equals 100 years, and "half a time" equals 50 years. The prophet Ezra began to write his books approximately 350 years before Rome defeated Greece in 146 BC. So God's timeline of the age given to Ezra provides additional credibility to the interpretation that 2,150 years is the meaning of "time, two times, and half a time."

Three Judgments

Figure 3 shows the 12 days of the present age as well as significant biblical and prophetic events occurring during

---

[118]   Spence, H.D.M. "Ezra." *The Pulpit Commentary*, Vol 7. Hendrickson Pub, 1985.

each thousand year day. The chart highlights seven times God made covenant with man, beginning with Adam and ending with the New Covenant, along with scripture references for each. In this chart, Adam and Eve are created on the sixth day of the age. God subsequently forms covenants with man seven different times. After man falls in the Garden of Eden, God executes three mighty judgments on the world.

The first is the Great Flood, which scholars believe occurred in approximately 2348 BC.[119] The Great Flood wiped out all humanity and left Noah and his family ruling the earth. Many Christians lose sight of the fact that great judgments of God are then followed by a remarkable transfer of authority to His children. The story of Noah provides perfect evidence. God gave Noah a command to build the Ark some 100 years before the Flood. The wicked around him ridiculed him mercilessly. Then Noah had the last laugh! God put Noah in charge of the entire world after this judgment.

The second major judgment came in the time of ancient Egypt. The biblical event of God's deliverance of Israel from Egypt provides the closest parallel to God's forthcoming judgment of the fourth beast. Pharaoh harnessed the anointing, creativity and sweat of God's people to become extraordinarily wealthy. Joseph interpreted Pharaoh's dream and then Pharaoh followed Joseph's recommendation to prepare for a famine. As a result, the entire world came to Egypt to buy food.

119   Wright, David. "Timeline for the Flood." *Answers in Genesis,* Accessed January 10, 2024. https://answersingenesis.org/bible-timeline/timeline-for-the-flood/

Figure 3: *Days of the Current Age, Followed by Stone Judgment and Kingdom Age of the Saints*

Day	Significant Biblical and Prophetic Events
1-6	- Undiscovered days of age. Potentially the first six days of creation in Genesis chapter 1 - 6th Day: Man created. God forms covenant with Adam and Eve[1]
7	- Man falls, yields authority to Satan. Expelled from Garden of Eden. God forms covenant with Adam (fallen man)[2]
8	- JUDGMENT #1: Great Flood - God forms covenant with Noah, who rules earth[3] - Nimrod reigns as first world leader in era of Tower of Babel - God forms covenant with Abram[4]
9	- Eqyptian empire under Pharaoh, Israelites enslaved - JUDGMENT #2: God delivers Israel, transfers wealth to them - God forms covenant with Moses[5] - Kingdoms of Israel and Judah established, first Temple built - God forms covenant with David[6]
10	- Babylonian empire begins, beginning times of Gentiles - First Temple destroyed under Babylon - Medo-Persia topples Babylon, Temple rebuilt - God announces New Covenant[7] - Greece topples Medo-Persia - Rome topples Greece, begins reign of fourth beast - Jesus Christ Born
11	- Jesus raised from dead. Gives followers spiritual authority over Satan. Restores relationship between God and Believers - Second Temple destroyed - Judaism perverted by Babylonian Talmud - Christianity perverted by Rome, who merges with Christianity (Roman Catholicism), quenching Christian revival - Rome revives into fourth beast system of nations
12	- Little horn (KM) subdues three nations of fourth beast, consolidates power through banking and finance system - Mass genocide between AD 1800-present, 25% of humanity destroyed - Holy Spirit awakening begins circa AD 1900 - 1 Billion babies aborted since AD 1920 - Fourth beast judged in Court of Heaven

JUDGMENT #3: Stone Judgment

Garden of Eden # Kingdom Age of the Saints *Rest*

7th Day of Humanity * 3rd Day of Church * 1st Chapter of New Age

1. Gen. 1:26-28 **2.** Gen. 3:14-19 **3.** Gen. 8:20-9:6 **4.** Gen. 12:1-3; 13:14-17; 15:1-7; 17:1-8 **5.** Ex. 20:1-31:18 **6.** 2 Sam. 7:4-17; 1 Chron. 17:4-15 **7.** Jer. 31:31-33; Matt. 26:28; Mark 14:24; Luke 22:20; Heb. 8:8-12

Egypt amassed a huge treasury of silver and gold. So large was Egypt's treasury that the Bible referred to the "gold of Egypt" several other times. Yet, when God delivered Israel from Egypt in a mighty judgment event, He transferred the Egyptian gold and silver to Israel in divine reparations for the 400+ years of slavery they endured. A few generations later, the people of Israel organized into a mighty kingdom, the wealthiest and most powerful kingdom at the time.

The third major judgment is the Stone Judgment, discussed in the book of Daniel chapter 2. The Stone Judgment ends the reign of tyranny of the fourth beast and ushers in an entirely new age. Daniel describes what he saw:

> As you watched, a rock was cut from a mountain,
> but not by human hands. It struck the feet of iron
> and clay, smashing them to bits. The whole statue
> was crushed into small pieces of iron, clay, bronze,
> silver, and gold. Then the wind blew them away
> without a trace, like chaff on a threshing floor. But
> the rock that knocked the statue down became a
> great mountain that covered the whole earth
> (Dan. 2:34-35 NLT).

Note the rock that destroys the statue becomes "a great mountain that covered the whole earth." In the Bible, mountains represent pillars of influence, or governments. A new government forms after the Stone Judgment, led by the saints of God. The rock that fills the earth also represents the glory of God.

7th Day Rest

The new age for mankind begins on the seventh day of mankind. God created man in the sixth day of the age. Man began in the Garden of Eden before falling. Man endured many ups-and-downs over the next 6,000 years. However, in the seventh day of humanity, God gives us rest. In the creation story in Genesis, God created the world in six days. On the seventh day, He rested:

> So the creation of the heavens and the earth and everything in them was completed. On the seventh day God had finished his work of creation, so he rested from all his work. And God blessed the seventh day and declared it holy, because it was the day when he rested from all his work of creation (Gen. 2:1-3 NLT).

God called the seventh day holy. God did not need to rest physically – He rested to enjoy His creation. As mentioned in Chapter 7, God promises in 2 Esdras 11:46 to "refresh" the earth after He judges the fourth beast. The Hebrew word for "refreshed" is the same word used in Exodus, "It is a permanent sign of my covenant with the people of Israel. For in six days the Lord made heaven and earth, but on the seventh day he stopped working and was refreshed" (v. 31:17).

I believe the seventh day of mankind is a prophetic day of rest. Just as God rested on the seventh day to enjoy His creation, He gives mankind a rest to enjoy God's creation. I remember traveling to Ethiopia several years ago and enjoying the most beautiful country I ever saw. On many mountaintops in Ethiopia, churches are carved out of solid rock to give glory to God. To access these churches, tourists typically hike up for about two hours to reach the sanctuaries. I remarked at the time, that the mountains and churches in Ethiopia were the "eighth wonder of the world" and asked our host why more people did not travel to Ethiopia to see them. She grimly replied, "Because of the constant turmoil in Ethiopia – we are a communist country." You see, the savage nature of the fourth beast not only routinely rapes and pillages countries of resources but they also install wicked governments that rob mankind of the ability to enjoy all of God's earth. Africa is quite possibly the most beautiful continent but it always seems to be wracked by war in at least a few regions simultaneously. In the Kingdom Age, we have peace and rest and are able to enjoy God's creation.

I call Hebrews 4 the "rest chapter." After a particularly grueling corporate battle ending in the market-value loss of my assets due to a greedy partner, I took a year off and dug into the Word of God. The Lord continually led me to Hebrews 4. I read the chapter hundreds of times! The other day, the Lord had me read it again. Armed with a fresh understanding of the next age, I realized the entire chapter is about the new age, and I missed it before! The chapter begins:

> The promise to enter the place of rest is still good,
> and we must take care that none of you miss out.
> We have heard the message, just as they did. But

they failed to believe what they heard, and the message did not do them any good. Only people who have faith will enter the place of rest. It is just as the Scriptures say, "God became angry and told the people, 'You will never enter my place of rest!' God said this, even though everything has been ready from the time of creation (Heb. 4:1-3 CEV).

The passage continues to describe how God rested the seventh day from all His works:

If Joshua had really given the people rest, there would not be any need for God to talk about another day of rest. But God has promised us a Sabbath when we will rest, even though it has not yet come. On that day God's people will rest from their work, just as God rested from his work (vv. 8-10).

In this amazing passage, the Bible points out during the Kingdom of Israel, when God's people ruled, Joshua failed to give Israel rest. David continually ran from King Saul, fought against Goliath, battled the Jebusites, and faced mutiny in his own kingdom. Despite being anointed king of Israel, David continually faced challenges. Times of peace proved fleeting for David. The passage also indicates that when Jesus came, *even He* did not bring a place of rest, for the scripture says "it has not yet come." Jesus gave His children authority over Satan, but not geopolitical authority. The fourth beast kept the true servants of God on-the-run and persecuted them for over two millennia. Even Jesus' own disciples suffered death at the hands of the fourth beast (except for John). Yes, a type of rest exists now, under the fourth beast system. We can rest in God's promises and in the favor of God, casting all worry aside. However, complete rest truly becomes available in the next age.

The true rest of God comes during the Kingdom Age of the Saints and the Millennial Reign of Christ, both chapters in the next age. When God rested after He created the world, He simply enjoyed His creation. A day comes soon when we can enjoy God's creation in the divine rest of God – the seventh day of mankind and the Kingdom Age of the Saints.

3rd Day Redemption

The Bible contains many references to rising up on the third day. Jesus provides the ultimate example – He went to the grave for two days and rose on the third day (Luke 24:7, 1 Cor. 15:4, Mark 9:31). As I pointed out, a day can mean a thousand years in scripture (2 Pet. 3:8). I believe Jesus rising on the third day represents a promise that the Church rises from under the thumb of the fourth beast after two days, or two thousand years. Let's look at additional scriptures and discuss their significance.

Jesus sent a message to Herod, the Rome-appointed King of Israel, "Go and say to that fox, Behold, I cast out demons and perform cures to-day and to-morrow, and the third *day* I am perfected" (Luke 13:32 ASV). Some translations say Jesus "finishes his course" on the third day.

In this rare statement, Jesus addresses Rome directly. He essentially said He would take authority over Satan and his forces for two days, and the third day His Body would be perfected. Most interpret this passage as another prophecy of Jesus' rising from the grave. However, during Jesus' two days in the grave, He was not casting out demons and performing cures. In fact, Jesus conducted important kingdom business while in paradise and he ultimately defeated Satan and took the keys of death and hell from him. As mentioned, the Body of Christ has possessed spiritual authority over Satan ever since Jesus came and possessed power to cast out demons and heal the sick in Jesus' name. However, at no point since Jesus' resurrection did the true Church possess geopolitical authority. Jesus may be speaking about the Kingdom Age of the Saints in the passage, where the Church rules the world, geopolitically, after Jesus "finishes" the Rome-rooted fourth beast and glorifies His Body.

Luke 24:7 says, "the Son of Man must be delivered into the hands of sinful men, and be crucified, and on the third day rise again." For 2,000 years, the Church was delivered into the hands of sinful men through persecution, martyrdom, and other grievous acts of the fourth beast. This passage indicates Jesus rises on the third day. Does the Church rise on the third day as well?

In Exodus 19:10-11 (ESV), the Lord said to Moses, "Go to the people and consecrate them today and tomorrow, and let them wash their garments and *be ready for the third day*. For on the third day the Lord will come down on Mount Sinai in the sight of all the people." Here the people of Israel needed to get ready to see God descend on Mount Sinai. They needed to sanctify, or set themselves apart (translated consecrate) to get ready to see God's glory. This process took two days, and the third day they were ready.

Jesus turned water into wine on the third day of the wedding in Cana (John 2:1-10). The fourth beast comes out of the sea (water), representing an evil cesspool of carnality and wickedness. Wine represents joy, celebration and festivity, expressing the abundant blessings of God. Jesus turned the water into wine on the *third day,* possibly representing the rest and abundance God promises in the Kingdom Age.

In Matthew 16:21, the Bible says, "From that time Jesus began to show his disciples that he must go to Jerusalem and suffer many things from the elders and chief priests and scribes, and be killed, and on the third day be raised." The fourth beast has toes of iron and clay, representing the government (iron) and clay (church). True saints of God suffered terribly under the hands of the organized church intermixed with government. In *KAS,* I discuss how in early efforts to achieve power under the fourth beast, Satan perverted Christianity and Judaism by hijacking them and intermixing them with idolatry. This not only weakened the power of the Gospel, but created a pseudo government-church bond that gave license for the organized church to reign terror on true Christians and Judeans. However, we see again that the third day brings victory.

In Hosea we read a powerful passage about a revival on the third day:

Come, and let us return unto the LORD: for he hath torn, and he will heal us; he hath smitten, and he will bind us up. After *two days* will he revive us: *in the third day* he will raise us up, and we shall live in his sight. Then shall we know, if we follow on to know the LORD: his going forth is prepared as the morning; and he shall come unto us as the rain, as the latter and former rain unto the earth (Hos. 6:1-3 KJV emphasis added).

The promise of revival on the third day aligns with the Stone Judgment in Daniel, when the blast of fire from God comes to the earth and ushers in God's presence (Dan. 7:9-11). Note the passage in Hosea discusses the latter *and* former rain. Rather than debate what this means, it looks like we get both in the third day!

"MENE, MENE…"

In Chapter 4, I discussed God's rebuke to the King of Babylon. The finger of God wrote on the walls during a pagan celebration the *very night* King Cyrus defeated King Balshazzar and brought down Babylon. The words written on the wall were, "MENE, MENE, TEKEL, UPHARSIN," translated by Daniel, "numbered, numbered, weighed, divisions." (See Dan. 5:25 AMPC). The reign of modern Babylon, extended nearly two-thousand years past Jesus' resurrection. Soon, we reach exactly two millennia. I believe the repeat of the word "MENE" twice indicates that God "weighs and divides" modern Babylon after two biblical days, or two thousand years. Judgment for Babylon came after King Belshazzar mocked God and drank from the golden Temple chalices. The tipping point for God's judgment of Pharaoh in Egypt came after Pharaoh began killing the children to "thin the herd" of the Israelites (see Ex. 1:22). The tipping point for judgment of the fourth beast includes mocking God and aborting over a billion children in the last 100 years. Soon God weighs and divides the fourth beast.

Lazarus "Sleeps"

When Jesus walked the earth, He met a lot of people but also held certain friends close. Jesus loved Lazarus, the brother of Mary of Bethany and Martha, as a friend. When Jesus heard that Lazarus died while He was on the road doing mission work, He said, "Lazarus's sickness will not end in death. No, it happened for the glory of God so that the Son of God will receive glory from this" (John 11:4 NLT). He then stayed where he was *two more days*. Then Jesus told His disciples, "Our friend Lazarus has fallen asleep, but now I will go and wake him up" (John 11:11). I believe God included this story in the Bible for the Church. First, Jesus said to His disciples, "You are my friends if you do what I command" (John 15:14). Any Christian following Jesus and His commands are friends with Him. So here we have a close friend of Jesus, Lazarus, dead. It's been two days and now Jesus says he sleeps.

The Church slept for two biblical days – two thousand years. After the early revival in the book of Acts, organized religion quenched the revival and removed the Bible from circulation to the general public for well over a thousand years. We finally got a Bible in our language, although this work is ongoing. The gifts of the Holy Spirit, including speaking with other tongues, recently reappeared on the scene in the Church at the turn of the 20ᵗʰ century. We saw glimpses of true revival in the last 120 years, but only for a few years at a time. The Church remained largely asleep for 2,000 years.

Note, Jesus says Lazarus' sickness (or sleep) will not end in death. What a promise! So many Christians out there believe the Church will be overpowered by the wicked forces ruling the world. Many believe, as I once did, that corrupt powers of this world may resort to locking up Christians in camps and committing genocide on God's people. Sadly, Christian genocide happened many times in our history. If you study *Fox's Book of Martyrs*, you read the alarming accounts of genocide of Christians occurring under the fourth beast, mostly at the hands of established religions or governments claiming to be "messengers of God."[120] God remembers every person destroyed on account of His name.

The physical sickness of Lazarus compares to the satanic sickness of the fourth beast – he hates Christians and also the seed of Jacob (see Rev 12). However, I bear good news. As Jesus said of Lazarus, the "sickness will not end in death," Jesus also says "it happened for the glory of God so that the Son of God will receive glory" (John 11:4). Unfortunately, man produced truckloads of bad doctrine derived from this scripture! However, the story of Lazarus

---

[120] Fox, John. *Fox's Book of Martyrs: History of the Lives, Sufferings and Triumphant Deaths, of the Primitive as Well as the Protestant Martyrs, from the Commencement of Christianity to the Latest Periods fo Pagan and Popish Persecutions.* Hurst & Co, 1870.

and the other accounts in the Bible related to rising on the third day are apocalyptic, prophetic glimpses. When God delivers His Church on the third day from the oppression and slavery of the fourth beast, He gets the glory.

Near the end of the story of Lazarus, Jesus discovers Lazarus has been dead for *four* days (John 11:17). If you go back four days in the days of the age, you find the Kingdom of Israel under King David. After God judged Egypt, He gave His people Israel a kingdom and they ruled. However, partial obedience of God's commandments and the worship of idols and other evil practices they learned in Egypt crept into their worship, and God took their kingdom from them. The church of the seed of Jacob, for lack of a better term, also "slept." Yet, there remained a remnant of the seed of Jacob that did, to the best of their ability, try to serve God. Many of these Judeans accepted Jesus as Messiah during His earthly ministry. Some failed to discover the Messiah but are scattered throughout the world. Regardless of whether they found our Messiah, they still suffered under the Khazarian Jews, Roman Catholics, Islamic groups and others who, influenced by Satan, tried to wipe them out in true anti-Semitism. However, God promised to preserve a remnant of the seed of Jacob. In Revelation 12, He shared that He would protect the seed of Mary (a descendant of the tribe of Judah) for a time, times and half a time, the duration of the Rome-rooted fourth beast. I believe the story of Lazarus shows that when Jesus raised up Lazarus after four days, He was showing us He plans to redeem the seed of Jacob during the Kingdom Age of the Saints.

Resurrection of the Body of Christ

The account of Jesus raising Lazarus from the dead in the book of John chapter 11 represents an incredible picture of when Jesus raises the Church from her "sleep." The name Lazarus, derived from the Hebrew name Eleazar, means "God has helped." For the Church, the transition to the Kingdom Age of the Saints involves a five step process:

1. *The stone needs to be rolled away.* The stone standing in the way of our resurrection is the fourth beast. The Stone Judgment destroys the fourth beast power structure.

2. *The sickness that caused us to "sleep" needs to be judged.* This includes judgment of the infiltrated church leaders, complicit in the evil corruption of the fourth beast. The sickness also includes the defiled government-religious bond. Jesus spoke to Lazarus in a loud, authoritative voice, "Lazarus, come forth!" Now He says, "True saints of God, come forth!"

3. *We need to be moved out of the grave.* After Jesus command, Lazarus supernaturally floated out of the grave, still bound. He could not walk, still bound in smelly linens. This supernatural act symbolizes the power of Jesus moving the Church into the next age. The stone in the Stone Judgment is made without hands.

4. *We need to be unwrapped.* Once out in the open, people needed to help Lazarus unwrap. There are Soldier Saints poised and ready to help the Church unwrap from the stiff chains that bind us. Awake Soldier Saints awaken sleeping saints. The Church emerges victorious and God "unwraps" our authority on earth.

5. *We need to be bathed in God's glory.* After the burial linens are removed, then we need a bath. The bath is the tangible presence and glory of God. God's glory filling the earth is a yet unfulfilled promise.

The story of Lazarus helps points to the Stone Judgment and the unwrapping of the Church. It's a better plan than we thought. When Jesus tells Martha her brother will rise again, she responds, "he will rise when everyone else rises, at the last day" (John 11:24). Today, most Christians believe nothing happens good for the Church until the "last day," when Jesus rules during the Millennial Reign of Christ. But Jesus planned a surprise for His friends – the resurrection of His Body, the Church!

The 4th Day

In *KAS,* I wrote that I believed the Kingdom Age of the Saints would last hundreds of years or more. I now see evidence that the first chapter in the next age might extend closer to 1,000 years. When the teachers of *religious law* (the Pharisees) asked Jesus to perform a special miracle or sign just for them to "prove His authority," Jesus gave a sharp rebuke. One Bible translation says they asked for His credentials. This group of authoritarians served Satan (John 8:44). They represented the fourth beast system, a merger of false religion and government. After Satan failed to convince Jesus to worship him in the desert, he worked through his agents in the fourth beast to try to get Jesus to submit to him. Notice what Jesus said in response to the Pharisees looking for a sign:

But Jesus replied, "Only an evil, adulterous generation would demand a miraculous sign; but the only sign I will give them is the sign of the prophet Jonah. For as Jonah was in the belly of the great fish for three days and three nights, so will the Son of Man be in the heart of the earth for three days and three nights (Matt. 12:39-40).

Jesus then reminded them of sinners in the past that recognized the day of their visitation from God and responded. The people of Ninevah and the Queen of Sheba both recognized God in the day of their visitation, but the secular fourth beast not only failed to recognize it, but repeatedly squashed any threats to its power.

Many Bible scholars remain confused about this passage, for it says Jesus will stay hidden for three days, not two – implying He would rise *on the fourth* day, not the third. To understand the sign, you must understand it was the only sign given to "that generation." Generation implies descent or progeny. Jesus essentially said, "I will be hidden to your progeny, your type, for three days." During the Kingdom Age, the Bible says that the children of Satan will not understand God's people (Dan 12:10). Jesus remains hidden from them for "another day." This would imply the Kingdom Age is 1,000 years, or another "day." Because when Jesus reappears He will be descending from Heaven with His saints during the battle of Armageddon (Rev 19:20-21). This is after the anti-Christ (the *fifth* beast) resurrects the image of the fourth beast, meaning he learned nothing after the Stone Judgment! (See Rev 13:11).

Dark Sun, Red Moon

In 2004, scientists discovered an asteroid over 300 meters across flies dangerously close to earth on April 13, 2029, just after the Jewish Passover.[121] Scientists named the asteroid Apophis, which ironically means "demon serpent of darkness," in ancient Egyptian mythology.[122] Scientists initially believed the asteroid would hit earth, inspiring several Hollywood films.

In Revelation 6, the sixth seal opens and the kings of the earth are judged by God. As explained in my first book, *KAS*, the sixth seal debunks most modern End Times teachings because the sixth seal falls *before* the seventh seal, which describes the Great Tribulation and the reign of the anti-Christ. Most traditional End Times teachings fail to explain the sixth seal, and instead point to the Battle of Armageddon as the next judgment event. I believe the sixth seal synonymous with the Stone Judgment prophesied in the book of Daniel chapter 2. The Stone Judgment represents the third major judgment of humanity and the major biblical event immediately preceding the Kingdom Age of the Saints (see Figure 3). The passage describing the sixth seal reads:

> When I saw the Lamb open the sixth seal, I looked and saw a great earthquake. The sun turned as

---

[121] "Apophis." *NASA*, Accessed January 30, 2024.
https://science.nasa.gov/solar-system/asteroids/apophis/

[122] "Apophis." *Collins Dictionary*, Accessed January 30, 2024.
https://www.collinsdictionary.com/us/dictionary/english/apophis#:~:text=(%C9%99%CB%88pouf%C9%AAs),Also%3A%20Apepi

dark as sackcloth, and the moon became as red as blood. The stars in the sky fell to earth, just like figs shaken loose by a windstorm. Then the sky was rolled up like a scroll, and all mountains and islands were moved from their places.

The kings of the earth, its famous people, and its military leaders hid in caves or behind rocks on the mountains. They hid there together with the rich and the powerful and with all the slaves and free people. Then they shouted to the mountains and the rocks, "Fall on us! Hide us from the one who sits on the throne and from the anger of the Lamb. That terrible day has come! God and the Lamb will show their anger, and who can face it (Rev 6:12-17 CEV)?

In the passage, evil kings of the earth are judged severely and hide in mountains. Could these be underground bunkers built by governments? The sun darkens and the moon turns red. Could the asteroid expected in AD 2029 cause these signs to occur in the sky? Time will tell. The timing of the expected asteroid occurs nearly exactly 2,000 years after the resurrection of Jesus, marking the end of the second biblical day and the beginning of the third. It also marks the beginning of the seventh biblical day for humanity, the day of rest.

Earlier in this chapter, I discuss the seventh "day of rest" that God took after He created the heavens and the earth. Given that a day with God represents a thousand years, the "day of rest" may also point to a thousand years for the Kingdom Age of the Saints. The end of the current age follows 12 parts, or days of the age, which I believe are 12,000 years. However, God created man on the sixth day of the age. So following the 12th day of the age, man would enter the seventh day following creation. I believe the seventh day represents a day of rest for mankind, likely lasting approximately 1,000 years.

Saints, just the thought of potentially being in a type of Garden of Eden for 1,000 years is exciting! It's the Church's time to shine. During the Kingdom Age, Jesus will perfect His Body as we prepare for the Marriage Supper of the Lamb.

10. The Man From the Sea

*I said, "O sovereign Lord, explain this to me: Why did I
see the man coming up from the heart of the sea?"*

– 2 Esdras 13:51 NRSV

In Chapter 4, I highlighted prophecies related to President
Trump by reputable and reliable prophets. The prophets
consistently refer to President Trump as both a modern-day
King Cyrus and also "God's David." In Isaiah 45, God gave
King Cyrus a special anointing to plow through unbreakable
barriers and humiliate the kings of the earth.

Of course, pundits point out the obvious: "If Trump represents Cyrus, why didn't he finish the job?" President Trump began a good work in his first term as U.S. president. However, it appeared that he surrounded himself with back-stabbers and blindly followed close relatives such as Jared Kushner into the "DC abyss." Dogged by the media every step of the way, President Trump did not *quite* get the border wall finished, for instance.

Now immigrants pour through the U.S. southern border like a sieve. Officially, *2.5 million* illegal immigrants crossed in 2023 by October, representing a new historic high.[123] The unofficial number likely far exceeds 2.5 million. So what's going on? I discovered a biblical passage that I believe points to President Trump in the Bible and also describes America's future. Fasten your seatbelts!

From the Heart of the Sea

Directly after the Lion judges the fourth beast in 2 Esdras 12, the Bible introduces us to a new character. This mysterious person develops into a great redeemer of humanity. Ezra describes seeing him in another dream:

> After seven days I dreamed a dream in the night. And lo, a wind arose from the sea and stirred up all its waves. As I kept looking the wind made something like the figure of a man come up out of the heart of the sea. And I saw that this man flew

[123] Putzel-Kavanaugh, Colleen & Ruiz Soto, Ariel G. "Shifting Patterns and Policies Reshape Migration to U.S.-Mexico Border in Major Ways in 2023." *Migration Policy Institute*, October 2023. https://www.migrationpolicy.org/news/border-numbers-fy2023#:~:text=The%202.5%20million%20encounters%20of,of%20year%2Dend%20government%20statistics.

with the clouds [or thousands] of heaven; and wherever he turned his face to look, everything under his gaze trembled, and whenever his voice issued from his mouth, all who heard his voice melted as wax melts when it feels the fire (2 Esdras 13:1-4 NRSV).

The Geneva Bible, an earlier translation, says "there was a mightie man" (old English spelling) to describe the "figure of a man" in the passage. We learn that the man comes up *from the sea*. As we discussed, the sea in the Bible represents the ungodly world system. So this mighty man comes out of the sea – out of the world's system.

President Trump made his fortune in the world. Before he ran for president, the world loved Donald Trump. He regularly interacted with Hollywood stars. Some of his earlier business ventures included casinos. For sure, Trump came out of the corrupt world system. In the passage we learn that everywhere the man looks his words invoke fear and people "feel the fire." We also learn that the man flies with the clouds of heaven or "thousands of heaven" (as translated in the King James Version and *The Geneva Bible*) who assist this man in his mission. This tells us that the host of heaven help this man fulfill his calling – literally thousands of angels help execute his plans. Many observe that President Trump endures incredible pressure from the media and lawsuits, yet always remains energetic. I believe he has an angelic host helping him.

Continuing in 2 Esdras 13, we learn the entire world tries to put this man down. Verse 5 says, "After this I looked and saw that an innumerable multitude of people were gathered together from the four winds of heaven to make war against the man who came up out of the sea." In the Bible, the term "four winds" describes the whole earth or heaven – all four corners of the earth (Jer. 49:36, Matt. 24:31). When the Bible uses "four winds," it usually describes something remarkable, unusual or devastating. The persecution and hatred the world currently exhibits toward President Trump exceeds the ordinary. President Trump endured two impeachment proceedings as president – a first in the history of the United States. In President Trump's first 100 days as president, CNN, NBC and CBS averaged over 90% negative coverage.[124] The relentless coverage of the Russia-Gate hoax began during the 2016 election cycle and continued until the Mueller report came out in April 2019. "Journalists" produced over 533,000 web articles and 2,284 minutes of Russia collusion broadcast news coverage on the Russia-Gate story.[125] This works out to roughly three minutes a night, *every night*, for 791 days.[126] Then the Mueller report came out and said, "The investigation did not establish that members of the Trump Campaign conspired or coordinated with the Russian government in its election interference

[124] Hunley, Steve. "Publishers Position." *The Knoxville Focus*, Accessed January 30, 2024. https://www.knoxfocus.com/archives/this-weeks-focus/harvard-study-confirms-trump-coverage/

[125] Serrano, Mark. "Four Lamest Excuses for the Media's Russia Coverage." *Real Clear Politics*, March 29, 2019. https://www.realclearpolitics.com/articles/2019/03/29/four_lamest_excuses_for_the_medias_russia_coverage_139893.html

[126] Noyes, Rich. "FIZZLE: Nets Gave Whopping 2,284 Minutes to Russia Probe." *mrcNewsBusters*, March 25, 2019. https://www.newsbusters.org/blogs/nb/rich-noyes/2019/03/25/fizzle-nets-gave-whopping-2284-minutes-russia-probe

activities," according to a quote by then Attorney General William Barr. The entire narrative painted by the media amounted to a sham and a witch-hunt.

In addition to character attacks by the media, the left launched a vindictive law-fare program (conducting warfare through bombarding your prey with lawsuits) against President Trump that would make the ACLU blush. New York Attorney General Letitia James, an elected Democrat, filed a lawsuit intended to destroy Trump's business empire.[127] Manhattan District Attorney Alvin Bragg, also an elected Democrat, indicted President Trump, charging him with 34 felonies related to the alleged hush money Trump arranged to pay porn star Stormy Daniels in the 2016 presidential campaign. Special counsel Jack Smith, appointed by the Biden Justice Department, began his investigation of President Trump in 2022 and indicted Trump over January 6 and the 2020 election in August 2023. Later, Smith indicted Trump in June of 2023 on 40 felony counts in the classified documents case. Fulton County District Attorney Fani Willis, an elected Democrat, indicted Trump on 13 felony counts relating to the 2020 election. D.C. Attorney General Karl Racine sued President Trump for his ownership in the Trump Hotel in Washington D.C., alleging he overcharged for events and enriched the president's family in the process, despite the hotel losing more than 70 million dollars during

[127] York, Byron. "Democratic lawfare vs. Donald Trump." *Washington Examiner,* December 20, 2023.
https://www.washingtonexaminer.com/daily-memo/2644325/democratic-lawfare-vs-donald-trump/

the four years of Trump's Presidency, including the years before pandemic shutdowns.[128]

When the Bible says the whole entire world tries to fight the man-from-the-sea, I believe this is fulfilled by what we have seen with President Trump. According to one news reporter, President Trump has survived "dozens" of legitimate attempts on his life with the only person surviving more attempts being Vladimir Putin.[129] While it's difficult to verify such information, I am certain we will one day confirm these as truth.

We discover more about the man-from-the-sea as we continue:

> After this I looked and saw that all who had gathered together against him to wage war with him were filled with fear, and yet they dared to fight. When he saw the onrush of the approaching multitude, he neither lifted his hand nor held a spear or any weapon of war, but I saw only how he sent forth from his mouth something like a stream of fire and from his lips a flaming breath and from his tongue he shot forth a storm of sparks.
>
> All these were mingled together, the stream of fire and the flaming breath and the great storm, and fell on the onrushing multitude that was

---

[128] AP. "Trump Hotel in D.C. officially gone, but Democrats don't want it entirely forgotten." *CBC,* May 14, 2022. https://www.cbc.ca/news/world/dc-trump-hotel-1.6450640

[129] Baxter, Michael. "Military Foils Another Plot to Assassinate President Trump." *Real Raw News,* June 26, 2023. https://realrawnews.com/2023/06/military-foils-another-plot-to-assassinate-president-trump/

prepared to fight and burned up all of them, so that suddenly nothing was seen of the innumerable multitude but only the dust of ashes and the smell of smoke. When I saw it, I was amazed (2 Esdras 13:8-11).

In the passage, we see that all who fight this man are filled with fear but still dare to fight. When one sees the incredible onslaught of attack against President Trump, one must conclude that President Trump knows where "the bodies are buried" in governments around the world. I believe this explains the fear President Trump's attackers possess, expressed in the passage. They know that President Trump could bury them with what he knows, so they must try to destroy him first.

In *KAS*, I mention that the little horn uses bribery and subterfuge to topple kingdoms in times of peace. The record of the bribes and crimes against humanity in the hands of a righteous person, are powerful. Note that the man in the passage does not "hold a spear or any weapon of war." He's a *civilian*, not a warrior like King David who led battles with weapons of warfare. This man fights back with his words, described as a "stream of fire" and "flaming breath," and from his tongue shot forth "a storm of sparks." Are these the "mean tweets?" Trump eviscerated opponents online, speaking truth about people in a way no recent U.S. president dared. Trump's "flaming breath" set off a firestorm of criticism and led to a whole industry of "fact checkers" that would wait for each new tweet and try to claim they were lies. Trump not only went against Democrats, but his *own* party, the Republicans. In 2021, *The New York Times* published, "The Complete List of Trump's Twitter Insults (2015-2021)," calling President Trump's tweets "verbal attacks."[130] It's one of the few articles from *The New York Times* that readers may access for free!

According to the passage in 2 Esdras, the battle between the man-from-the-sea and his opponents moves beyond the realm of "mean tweets." A "great storm" ensues and the man-from-the-sea falls on the multitude prepared to fight and utterly and completely defeats them. In a meeting with military leaders in 2017, President Trump warned of "the calm before the storm." When asked what he meant, President Trump replied, "You'll find out!"[131] The passage indicates after the "great storm," there is nothing left of the "innumerable multitude" but dust of ashes and the smell of smoke. But how does this happen?

The Final Battle

In Chapter 8, I lay out how the three-headed eagle perishes. The three-headed eagle represents the final leadership of the fourth beast, a triune nation-state that operates as one to fulfill the wishes of the little horn, the KM. The Bible says that the fourth beast is judged by the Ancient of Days (God) in the Court of Heaven (Dan. 7:26). And the Bible gives us the

---

[130] Quealy, Kevin. "The Complete List of Trump's Twitter Insults (2015-2021)." *The New York Times,* January 19, 2021. https://www.nytimes.com/interactive/2021/01/19/upshot/trump-complete-insult-list.html

[131] Calfas, Jennifer. "President Trump Warns of 'the Calm Before the Storm' during military meeting." *Time,* October 5, 2017. https://www.time.com/497138/donald-trump-calm-before-the-storm-military-white-house.

actual conversation that occurs in 2 Esdras 11:38-46, where Jesus (the Lion) delivers the message to the fourth beast. Once the Most High judges the fourth beast, he dies slowly at first, then suddenly. A delay exists between the initial judgment of the fourth beast and his death, during which time the three nation-states fight and kill each other. The book of Revelation also describes a civil war among the participating nations of the fourth beast system in Revelation 17:16-17. We learn more about the tactics of the battle in 2 Esdras 13, when the man-from-the-sea defeats the nations of the fourth beast who line up to fight him – afraid.

In 2 Esdras 13:6, we learn the man-from-the-sea flies into a mysterious mountain. Verses 6-7 say, "And I looked and saw that he carved out for himself a great mountain and flew up on to it. And I tried to see the region or place from which the mountain was carved, but I could not." We learn the man-from-the-sea carves out the mountain for himself. Could this be Mount Cheyenne, the military complex that President Trump placed under the United States Space Force command in early 2020?[132] Based on the order of the verses in 2 Esdras 13, it appears that after the man-from-the-sea flies upon the mountain, then the actual fight breaks out.

Recall from Chapter 6, where I mention that former *Forbes* journalist Benjamin Fulford received information from his sources that the real President Trump flew to Mount Cheyenne years ago for protection. Could he have staged a military operation from Cheyenne Mountain to take

---

[132] Woody, Christoper. "The US Air Force finally has a Space Force, and now some of its bases could be getting new names." *Business Insider,* January 7, 2020.
https://www.businessinsider.com/air-force-bases-renamed-as-part-of-space-force-creation-2020-1

down the KM and other deep state operators? Without proper clearance, I could not possibly verify this information. I could be wrong, but I believe the man-from-the-sea in 2 Esdras represents President Trump. The deep state still controls assets worldwide and if President Trump were staging military actions against the deep state, he would not be safe until all deep state assets are eliminated or incarcerated.

The methods with which the man-from-the-sea wages war are explained in 2 Esdras 13:37-39 where it discusses the three methods employed:

> Then he, my Son, will reprove the assembled nations for their ungodliness (this was symbolized by the storm) and will reproach them to their face with their evil thoughts and the torments with which they are to be tortured (which were symbolized by the flames) and will destroy them without effort by means of the law (which was symbolized by the fire).

When I first saw "Son" capitalized, I confused the man-from-the-sea with Jesus. However, Jesus would not be described as the "man from the sea." As already explained, the sea in the Bible represents worldly evil, and is where the whore of Babylon resides. To ascribe Jesus to the sea would represent apostasy and denial of the Virgin Birth.

Note in the passage the man-from-the-sea reproves nations, plural. This indicates the battle to destroy the fourth beast rages internationally and involves many (if not all) nations, not just the United States. The storm represents the exposure of ungodliness. The exposure going on right now in the media remains unprecedented. The Bible says all things done in darkness will be exposed – happening right now. For the first time in our lifetimes, we see great exposure of the deep state: Epstein flight logs, false Israel, media lies, fraudulent medical-establishment, corrupt military-industrial-complex and related money-laundering by politicians, for example. The ongoing exposure represents a foretaste of coming judgment of pedophiles and other people committing crimes against humanity.

Finally, the destruction by means of the law describes the military tribunals and other criminal trials to occur for the fourth-beast-enablers. I believe the civilian courts of law are insufficient for the task of bringing the fourth beast minions to justice. The civilian halls of justice prove corrupt and subject to delays and manipulation by embedded fourth-beast-judges. The fourth beast held control of humanity for thousands of years and owns the civilian court system. For the man-from-the-sea to achieve justice, he must use fast-acting military justice, according to the military war manual.

Near-Death Experience for Humanity

According to 2 Esdras, before the man-from-the-sea comes on the scene, the fourth beast *planned* great destruction. I believe the enemy planned to launch World War III and do their best to eliminate the majority of the population. Consider this passage:

> The days are coming when the Most High will deliver those who are on the earth. And bewilderment of mind shall come over those who inhabit the earth. They shall plan to make war against one another, city against city, place against place, people against people, and kingdom against kingdom. When these things take place and the signs occur that I showed you before, then my Son will be revealed, whom you saw as a man coming up from the sea (2 Esdras 13:29-32).

Several years ago, I began to study the plans of the enemy and realized their intentions to destroy humanity. I became a doomsday prepper, believing evil possessed sufficient power and control over the planet to achieve their goal of total destruction. The fourth beast *did* craft plans to destroy humanity. But God judged the fourth beast in the Court of Heaven and raised up a man "coming up from the sea" to foil their plans. Let me be clear, when the smoke clears only God gets the glory. I believe God released His plan to deliver humanity to the minds of man many decades ago, and literally thousands of men and women banded together to fulfill God's plan. I believe the military asked President Trump to fulfill a role and purpose, and he answered the call. In the battle against evil, many world leaders are involved, including Trump, Putin, Modi, Xi and others. Also, many military forces are involved – not just the U.S. military.

Thankfully, the world recognized the depths of evil planned for humanity and our true enemy, the KM. This tribe of evildoers and Satan-worshippers planned the destruction of the world. People in Russia remember the tyranny that communism produced under Lenin and Stalin – grandfathers and grandmothers resorted to cannibalism to survive the misery. Citizens of China remember the treachery of Mao and the extreme poverty and genocide caused by tyranny. Parents across the world lost sons and daughters to pointless wars fought for bankers. Families lost loved ones who lost their lives preaching the Gospel in remote parts controlled by mobsters who introduced civil unrest into African nations simply to control the natural resources. The world woke up to the nature, methods and means of our true enemy. Now, the world alliance unites to bring him down. Glory to God!

The Smoke Clears

When the battle is over, the man-from-the-sea serves a unique role for humanity. He takes on a special role that we should be prepared for – a type of king. Listen to the passages in 2 Esdras 13:

> This is the interpretation of the vision: As for your seeing a man come up from the heart of the sea, this is he whom the Most High has been keeping for many ages [or "great season"], who will himself deliver his creation, and he will direct those who are left (vv. 25-26).
>
> Therefore when he destroys the multitude of the nations that are gathered together, he will

> defend the people who remain. And then he will
> show them very many wonders (vv. 49-50).

Most translations say that God keeps the man-from-the-sea for a "great season." (As I explained earlier, age is mistranslated in many translations). God planned to install the man-from-the-sea at the right time. This verse shows the divine nature of God, that He knows people before they are born. In Jeremiah 1:5, God says to Jeremiah, "Before I formed you in the womb I knew you, and before you were born I consecrated you; I appointed you a prophet to the nations." God knows about us and the plans He has for us *before we are born*. This should settle forever the abortion debate!

In the passage, God says the man-from-the-sea will "deliver his creation." God uses the man-from-the-sea to deliver the earth and humanity from the fourth beast. The fourth beast's plans to destroy humanity fail, and efforts to poison the planet fall apart. Next, we learn the man-from-the-sea will "direct those who are left." According to the *Concise Oxford English Dictionary*, the word "direct" means to control the operations of, or supervise and control, or give an order to. In the second passage, he serves to "defend" the people that remain. I believe Trump takes on a larger role than simply president of the United States, although he may also serve in this capacity. Trump may end up as a king in the Kingdom Age of the Saints.

We should recognize that after we root out the evil mafia who ruled the world for thousands of years, Satan remains loose. Satan is not bound until the Millennial Reign of Christ. We will need someone to help us "mind the garden" and stamp out any remnant of evil that raises its ugly head during the Kingdom Age. I hope the Church one day steps into the role, but I also recognize how easily Satan fooled the Church over the last 2,000 years. I believe we need an awake leader to help us put down infiltrators during the Kingdom Age – Trump could fulfill this role. When Trump steps into the role, he will show us what the alliance discovered underground during the battle against the fourth beast. He also shows humanity what's in store – a time of great prosperity and abundance. Finally, the "hidden manna" of Revelation 2:17 will be revealed.

When the man-from-the-sea addresses the multitudes after coming out of the mountain, we learn about his interaction with humanity – now set free:

> After this I saw the same man come down from the mountain and call to himself another multitude that was peaceable. Then many people came to him, some of whom were joyful and some sorrowful; some of them were bound, and some were bringing others as offerings (2 Esdras 13:12).

The man-from-the-sea then assembles the people. Four groups of people come:

1. *Joyful* – These are the patriots thrilled with justice and happy to see their man, Trump, victorious. These are the digital warriors who fought to expose evil. These are the intercessory prayer warriors. These are the political prisoners

locked up for exposing the government corruption. These are the fearless military soldiers who risked their lives to destroy enemy fortresses. These are the Soldier Saints.

2. *Sorrowful* – Some are sad to see the fourth beast system go. The system enriched them and now they live in a new world with different rules. They are full of sorrow and miss the old system.

3. *Bound* – Captured criminals are punished. They face public humiliation, disgrace and judgment for their criminal acts in the fourth beast regime.

4. *Whistle-blowing* – These are people caught up in the fourth beast system that will try to cut leniency deals by offering to turn state's evidence on others. Some deals maybe necessary, but my hope is that all criminals face severe punishment. We must not allow evil into the new system.

The dawn of the Kingdom Age of the Saints brings great joy for the vast majority of the world. The tyranny of the fourth beast created generational enemies and killed and hurt billions of people – most are thrilled the old system blows up. However, the new system represents great change. The change requires great adjustment. All the systems we rely on today eventually give way to a brand new system. Change proves difficult for most, particularly older people. Allow God to prepare your heart now.

Peace for Israel

When the man-from-the-sea addresses the people, he stands on Mount Zion. In the Bible, Zion refers to where God dwells and reigns. It's not necessarily the city of Jerusalem, although the city of Jerusalem remains special to God. For we read in Isaiah 62:1, "For Zion's sake will I not hold my peace, and for Jerusalem's sake I will not rest, until the righteousness thereof go forth as brightness, and the salvation thereof as a lamp *that* burneth" (KJV). The Hebrew origin of the name Zion means "highest point." In the New Testament, Zion refers to God's Kingdom. So when the man-from-the-sea stands on Mount Zion, he is representing God's Kingdom on earth. Let's read a couple more passages in 2 Esdras 13:

> But he shall stand on the top of Mount Zion. And Zion shall come and be made manifest to all people, prepared and built, as you saw the mountain carved out without hands (vv. 35-36 NRSV).
>
> And as for your seeing him gather to himself another multitude that was peaceable, these are the nine tribes [or ten, based on translation] that were taken away from their own land into exile in the days of King Hoshea, whom Shalmaneser, king of the Assyrians, made captives; he took them across the river, and they were taken into another land (vv. 39-40).
>
> Then they lived there until the last times, and now, when they are about to come again, the Most High will stop the channels of the river

again, so that they may be able to cross over. Therefore you saw the multitude gathered together in peace. But those who are left of your people, who are found within my holy borders, shall be saved (vv. 46-48).

It's significant that the nine (or ten) tribes are mentioned in the passage. I assume these are nine (or ten) "lost" tribes of the twelve tribes of Israel, the seed of Jacob. It appears the "lost" tribes of Jacob may return to Jerusalem. Verse 48 mentions that those "left of your (Hebrew) people, who are found within my holy borders, shall be saved." This tells me the area around Palestine and Israel will be seized from the KM. The seed of Jacob may then live where they want – some will go back to Israel. We may also see the continents begin to drift closer together, when God "stops the channels of water."

Peace for America

America – the land of the free and home of the brave. The place where dreams come true. People from all over the world found freedom from tyranny in America. The early Pilgrims faced hardships but they stood strong because they trusted in our Lord. As we read in the Mayflower Compact, they dedicated their efforts and government to God. Is God done with America because we as a nation served under the little horn who used our children to fight wars for the bankers? No. God remembers America for William Bradford, for Thomas Jefferson, for George Washington and others. Just as He blessed ancient Israel for King David's sake, His blessing rests on America for the early founders' sake.

In 2 Esdras 13, America is mentioned (Arzareth) in an account that offers both historical context on the past, as well as prophesies a future, parallel event:

> But they formed this plan for themselves, that they would leave the multitude of the nations and go to a more distant region, where no human beings had ever lived, so that there at least they might keep their statutes that they had not kept in their own land. And they went in by the narrow passages of the Euphrates river. For at that time the Most High performed signs for them, and stopped the channels of the river until they had crossed over. Through that region there was a long way to go, a journey of a year and a half; and that country is called Arzareth (vv. 41-45).

1. Historical Account of Past Scattering: The ancient nine (some translations say ten) tribes of the Northern Kingdom of Israel, scattered after the siege of Assyria (Jer. 31:8, Isa. 11:12, Ezek. 20:21-24, 1 Kings 14:14-16). Many historical maps and accounts of the region of Great Tartaria mention the ten tribes of Israel once occupied territory located in modern-day eastern Europe and Russia.[133] It is thought that at least some of the group passed east into America in a time when the continents more closely aligned. Researchers discovered

---

[133] "Map of the Great Tartary. Established upon the Accounts of Several Travelers from Various Nations and Several Observations Made in that Country." *Library of Congress,* 1757. https://lccn.loc.gov/2021668613

Hebrew practices in the native tribes of America. Thomas Jefferson famously quoted the beliefs of James Adair, a researcher who lived among the Native Americans for 40 years, in a letter to John Adams in June 1812, stating Adair's observation: "...all the Indians of America to be descended from the Jews: the same laws, usages, rites & ceremonies, the same sacrifices, priests, prophets, fasts and festivals, almost the same religion, and that they all spoke Hebrew."[134] Christopher Columbus, a student of the Bible, identified America with the name Azareth, recognizing that Hebrew tribes lived in America.[135]

2. Future Prophecy Concerning Pilgrims: Over 2,000 years ago, Ezra prophesied about another group that would travel to America for religious freedom. The time between the initial land-patent grant in June of 1619 until the Pilgrims decided to settle the hill in Plymouth in 1621 spanned exactly 18 months (see Chapter 2). In addition, the Pilgrims left Holland for the same reason as the lost tribes of Israel, although this time to practice their Christian faith free from government intervention.

Both groups came to America for religious freedom. It is widely believed that the ten tribes of Israel scattered many other places as well, including South America, Cuba, Australia, and Mexico. Most of the true seed of Jacob likely recognized Jesus as The Messiah. In any case, the man-from-the-sea gathers the "multitude that was peaceable,"

---

[134] Adams, John. "Thomas Jefferson to John Adams, 11 June 1812." *National Archives,* June 11, 1812. https://founders.archives.gov/documents/Jefferson/03-05-02-0100

[135] Kayserling, Meyer. *Christopher Columbus and the Participation of the Jews in the Spanish and Portuguese Discoveries.* (Forgotten Books, 2012). 15.

representing the lost tribes of Israel, as well as others, and "shows them very many wonders."

In the Kingdom Age, I believe we restore America to the Constitutional Republic, devoid of foreign interests. However, we must understand God's plan involves restoring *all* humanity in the Kingdom Age – worldwide. All "sheep" nations chose to participate in the Kingdom Age economy, full of freedom and prosperity. There will exist "goat" nations who reject God's government and remain in isolation. Some nations choose to be under a benevolent and rightful king or queen. Others adopt new constitutional republics. I believe it will be up to the people in each nation to choose their form of local government.

Better for Those "Left Behind"

As Ezra processed the dream God gave him, he recognizes something that confuses him. After seeing God judge the fourth beast, Ezra knew the age of tyranny ends. He then sees the man-from-the-sea defeat the nations and establish peace and show the peaceable assembly many wonders, too great for him to process in his mind.

The mountain made without hands destroys the statue in Daniel's night vision and fills the whole earth, representing a new pillar of authority within the earth – God's Kingdom (Dan 2:34-35). I believe God also showed Ezra how His glory would fill the earth. The blast of fire from God's throne judges the fourth beast and ushers in great revival for the Church (Dan 9:9-11). "And Zion shall come and be made manifest to all people, prepared and built, as you saw the mountain carved out without hands" (2 Esdras 13:35 NRSV). Notice the pillar of authority, the mountain from Heaven, the Kingdom Age of the Saints is already "prepared and built." The work of creating the technology, processes and laws for the Kingdom Age started years ago. Soldier Saints quietly built these systems for decades. When revealed to mankind, it's already "prepared and built." However, the man-from-the-sea rolls it out!

The goodness of God, the glory manifest among the people, the refreshing of the earth, the return to the Garden of Eden, is all too much for Ezra to process. He exclaims:

> Then I woke up in great terror and prayed to the Most High and said, "From the beginning you have shown your servant these wonders and have deemed me worthy to have my prayer heard by you; now show me the interpretation of this dream also. For as I consider it in my mind, alas for those who will be left in those days! And still more, alas for those who are not left!
>
> For those who are not left will be sad because they understand the things that are reserved for the last days but cannot attain them. But alas for those also who are left and for that very reason! For they shall see great dangers and much distress, as these dreams show.
>
> Yet it is better to come into these things, though incurring peril, than to pass from the world like a cloud and not to see what will happen in the last days (2 Esdras 13:13b-20).

God interprets and adds to Ezra's observation:

> As for what you said about those who survive, and concerning those who do not survive, this is the interpretation: The one who brings the peril at that time will protect those who fall into peril, who have works and faith toward the Almighty. Understand, therefore, that those who are left are more blessed than those who have died (2 Esdras 13:22-24).

In a wild statement of awe, Ezra points out that the people that make it into the Kingdom Age of the Saints are *more blessed* than the people who have already died! Glory to God! Ironically, the *Left Behind* movie series, starring Kirk Cameron, portrays the exact opposite.[136] We are taught that the world gets progressively worse and then – poof! Christians fly to Heaven in the Rapture. In the movies, those left behind experience brutal persecution and many die. The reality in God's Word is the world gets worse and *then* we move into the Kingdom Age on the earth!

Ezra sees that humanity's best days are after the end of the old age under the oppression of the fourth beast system, and that even the people already dead wish they experienced this time! In the passage in 2 Esdras, we see the time preceding the Kingdom Age fraught with peril and danger. Earlier, we learned our enemy schemed to wreak more havoc and destruction. The enemy's plans are interrupted, however. God judges the fourth beast, and then puts His man in place

---

[136]   Sorbo, Kevin. Baxley, et. al., director. *Left Behind (Series)*. Paul Lalonde, 1994-2023.

to take down the corrupted nations – the man-from-the-sea, whom I believe is Donald J. Trump.

11. Kingdom Age Destiny

Michael, the chief of the angels, is the protector of your people, and he will come at a time of terrible suffering, the worst in all of history. And your people who have their names written in The Book will be protected.

– Daniel 12:1 CEV

After I received the revelation of the Kingdom Age of the Saints in late 2022, I felt led to write a book to help the Church understand God's magnificent plan. I planned to use a pen name. Up to that point, I principally used my gifts in the area of business, starting and launching several companies. Books about how Satan infiltrated Christianity, Judaism and government are unpopular in business circles. What's more, the revelation of the Kingdom Age flies in the face of thousands of books written on End Times, potentially starting a war within religious circles in the Church. Recently, I bought a copy of *KAS* for someone else and the bookseller showed me other books people bought at the same time. When I saw the list, I realized that *KAS* contradicts the vast majority of traditional books people bought on eschatology. Anticipating this, I planned to use a pen name and "drop the microphone" – anonymously.

After several days of fasting for unrelated reasons, I felt the urge by the Holy Spirit to use my real name. The decision created strife in my household while other friends called and congratulated me on the decision. Based on what I later discovered in God's word, I now understand the importance of my choice to write *KAS* under my actual name. Calling out tyranny can be a lonely place. Most Christians and humanity in general prefer a "happy place." However, we live in a unique time.

The transition to the Kingdom Age involves warfare and judgment, and God calls us to participate. There are times when Christians need to suit up and fight tyranny – this is one of those times. I firmly believe our lethargy in the Church kept us out of the fight against a cultural takeover of Satan of the seven pillars of society. What's worse, our bad doctrine related to the Rapture gave us the justification to do absolutely nothing about the cultural decline.

While society burned, most Christians stood on the sideline. We failed to show up at school board meetings, run for office, or use our voice in our communities. The organized church adopted as doctrine the idea that the world continued to get worse, then God "rescues" Christians in a rapture event. This doctrine alleviated any and all responsibility of Christians to get involved. If the place burns up anyway, why bother? Unfortunately, many gifts and dreams also remained hidden. This ploy of the enemy rendered the Church ineffective against the tide of evil overpowering our world. The Church lost its voice – we didn't fight. Then we woke up and wondered: "How did things get so bad?" Satan knows his time is short, and he plotted, schemed and marched toward world domination, destroying everything good and beautiful along the way.

God plans to redeem His Church by giving us an opportunity to reign in the Kingdom Age. However, He will use those courageously operating in their gifts and talents the most. When unbelievers arrive at the judgment seat in the Great White Throne Judgment, they won't be judged about whether they made mistakes in the flesh. Listen to this passage in Revelation:

> I saw the dead, both great and small, standing before God's throne. And the books were opened, including the Book of Life. And the dead were judged according to what they had done, as recorded in the books (Rev 20:12 NLT).

Have you ever wondered what book God uses to judge the dead? Most picture a mysterious and large book that God keeps in Heaven. Years ago, I saw a hand-written detailed accounting ledger for the first time and thought to myself, "I think that's what the Book of Life looks like!" God is 100% just. He's not planning to judge people based on a book they never saw. I believe the Book of Life *is* the Bible. Note the passage says the dead are judged "according to what they had done, as recorded in the books." In other words, they are judged based on whether they fulfilled their calling, as outlined in the Bible.

You see, everyone that achieved great things found themselves in the Bible and then operated in the authority of knowing their calling. In Chapter 2, I discuss how Christopher Columbus discovered himself in the Bible. In fact, Columbus wrote an entire book where he detailed the scriptures he believed he partially fulfilled. We don't know whether the Pilgrims discovered themselves in the Bible. However, we do know the Bible version they carried on the Mayflower, *The Geneva Bible,* contained the passage we read in the last chapter from 2 Esdras, where a people seeking to worship God left their land and traveled 18 months to seek a new land where they could worship freely. I feel certain that God showed William Bradford the passage in 2 Esdras.

Given the Pilgrims' voyage succeeded Christopher Columbus' own voyage to the new world, the Pilgrims' own maps most likely listed Arzareth on the map. It's also likely the Pilgrims knew they were the second group fleeing to the Americas for religious freedom. Knowing God's specific plan in the Word of God gives a person supernatural confidence and courage to fulfill his calling. Soldier Saints know where they are in the Bible. Let's find out how to discover yourself in the Bible!

Clue #1 – Your First Name

In Hebrew times, men and women were known by their first name. For instance, people knew Solomon as the "son of David." In modern times, we use last names to help identify people. When I discovered myself in the Bible, my first name, Benjamin, led me there.

Earlier I mentioned that I planned to use a pen name on my first book, *KAS*. I selected for my pen name "Conor Gloriam" – words in Latin translated "follow the glory." I proudly put it on the book draft. However, when the Lord spoke to me, I felt Him say: "Use your own name. I plan to give further revelation from My Word to Benjamin, not Conor." God rejected my pen name! He wanted me to go with the name my parents gave me. My parents happened to be Believers when they named me, so perhaps that mattered. But I believe that God easily overcomes the hurdle of unbelieving parents. He can speak through pagan kings and even used a mule to prophesy. I believe the name we are given at birth matters. If your name was changed for any reason, find out your original birth name and start there.

Find the Hebrew or Greek root of your first name. List all the scriptures that mention your given name. Ask God to show you which ones apply. You might be drawn to a certain character, for instance. Many in the Bible raised their children right and later they became mighty prophets. Others were blessed to house men and women of God in their homes. Of course, others went into ministry. If you ask God to show you, He is faithful.

Let's talk about a couple of people in the Bible who discovered themselves. An angel showed Mary and Joseph what to name Jesus. His Hebrew name would be pronounced, "Yeshua." (In prayer, I address Him by this name). Yeshua literally means "Savior." The second major act of obedience for Mary and Joseph included naming Jesus what God intended. As a young boy, Jesus studied the Bible and found himself in there; He knew all the passages where He was listed. In fact, in His first sermon He read from Isaiah 61, which says:

> The Spirit of the Lord God is upon me, because the Lord has anointed me to bring good news to the poor; he has sent me to bind up the brokenhearted, to proclaim liberty to the captives, and the opening of the prison to those who are bound; to proclaim the year of the Lord's favor (vv. 1-2a ESV).

Following Jesus' first sermon, He "began to say to them, 'Today this Scripture has been fulfilled in your hearing'" (Luke 4:21). You see, Jesus discovered Himself in God's Word. Jesus *did not* quote the whole passage when he preached out of Isaiah 61. For the next verses dealt with a day of vengeance that was not to come until 2,000 years later – the Stone Judgment. Jesus knew which Bible verses He was in the act of fulfilling, and which came later. Jesus' own name – Yeshua, Savior, guided Him to find Himself in the Word of God.

John the Baptist also discovered himself in the Bible. When asked who he was, "John replied in the words of the prophet Isaiah: 'I am a voice shouting in the wilderness, 'Clear the way for the LORD's coming!'" (John 1:23 NLT). At some point, John discovered who he was in scripture and headed out to the desert to begin his ministry. Note in John's case, it does not say "John" in Isaiah 40:3, the verse John quoted. It simply says, a "voice." Yet, John knew Isaiah spoke of a future person who would announce the coming of the Savior. When you search for yourself in the Word of God, you might not find your name, but God will show you the scripture you are intended to fulfill if you ask Him.

Listen to the words of Jesus in Revelation, "Everyone who wins the victory will wear white clothes. Their names will not be erased from the book of life, and I will tell my Father and his angels that they are my followers" (Rev 3:5 CEV). The Book of Life, the Bible, contains God's calling on our lives. We choose to step into and follow that calling. If we don't, I believe someone else takes our place. For instance, I believe God called President Trump to be the man-from-the-sea and usher in the Kingdom Age. However, if President Trump refused this call, then God would use someone else. God's timetable for humanity is perfect.

God calls people for "such as time as this." Listen to what Mordecai told Esther, when the entire Hebrew race was under threat of eradication during the reign of Xerxes (a Persian King). "For if you keep silent at this time, *relief and deliverance will rise for the Jews from another place*, but you and your father's house will perish. And who knows whether you have not come to the kingdom for such a time as this?" (Est. 4:14 ESV, emphasis added). Mordecai told Esther if she did not obey, then she and her father's house would die and the deliverance of the Jews would come from another place. You see, Mordecai knew the promise to Israel, and he sensed God calling Esther to step up and lead. But God would not force Esther to obey. If Esther failed to answer the call, she would be murdered and Esther's name would be blotted out of the Book of Life – there would be no book of Esther in the Bible for us to read today.

In the same way Mordecai warned Esther, the military likely warned President Trump he could die if he failed to accept the assignment. At any point, President Trump could back out of the job. If he backs out, God will use someone else.

As we enter the Kingdom Age of the Saints, it's critical for Soldier Saints to step up to the plate. Things are accelerating and God is choosing His leaders for the next age now. The sooner we discover ourselves in the Bible and act on our assignments, the sooner we enter our high calling.

Clue #2 – Your Inner Desires

My pastor in New York used to say, "The Holy Spirit and my wife sound a lot alike." It made people laugh, but he acknowledged the Lord frequently used his wife to speak to him, and her voice agreed and confirmed the Holy Spirit's direction. I found that my desires and interests and calling sound a lot alike. For instance, I loved business at a young age. Even though I studied engineering and earned a science degree, my heart remained in business – I practiced engineering for only a year. Over the next 20 years, I thrived in business (most of the time) and God blessed me with the ability to give substantially to Kingdom works. I recognized God's gift in me to see things others didn't and I typically went into industries before the masses recognized their significance. "Seeing into the future" represented a gift from God. It is a gift that I used in business, but now am applying to teaching God's Word.

God gave each of us deep-down desires. I am not speaking about desires of the flesh, such as lust, greed, covetousness, etc. Psalm 37:4 says, "Delight yourself in the LORD, and he will give you the desires of your heart." When we delight in the Lord and spend time with Him, He loves to give us the desires of our heart. In *Kingdom Age of the Saints: Study Guide & War Manual,* I present a template for readers to put together their humanitarian plan to bless humanity, assuming unlimited resources. As I put my plan together, I realized that my interests and my plan aligned. For instance, I am very interested in healthy food, clean air, and clean water. Our family eats organic foods and I enjoy studying farming methods, water purification techniques, and using microbes to clean up toxins in our soil. Because of this interest, a number of my humanitarian plans focus on these areas. We work harder and are more motivated in areas we enjoy. These are God-given desires.

It's time for Soldier Saints to dig out old dreams, plans, visions and desires. When we get to Heaven, we will find our mansions are built exactly to reflect our desires. The furniture, the colors, everything down to the smallest detail reflects our personal tastes. Our Lord cares about the smallest details – He's that good. Be in tune with your desires. If you are in a job that you hate, ask the Lord for a job you love and start looking. I believe it's critical to enter the Kingdom Age knowing who you are and what work you would like to engage in for the Kingdom. If you check your heart, however, and find greed and covetousness there, get it out. Learn to love to help people – for this is the heart of God. "But seek first the kingdom of God and his righteousness, and all these things will be added to you" (Matt. 6:33-34).

Clue #3 – Your Gifts

In Ephesians 4, Paul writes about how after Jesus ascended after His crucifixion, He unlocked gifts for each man or woman:

> Yet grace (God's unmerited favor) was given to each of us individually [not indiscriminately, but in different ways] in proportion to the measure of Christ's [rich and bounteous] gift. Therefore it is said, When He ascended on high, He led captivity captive [He led a train of vanquished foes] and He bestowed gifts on men [Ps. 68:18] (vv. 7-8 AMPC).

Armed with the Blood of Jesus, fellowship with the Holy Spirit, and the promises in God's Word, each of us should know our gifting. Your gifts can't be taken away, "For God's gifts and His call are irrevocable. [He never withdraws them when once they are given, and He does not change His mind about those to whom He gives His grace or to whom He sends His call]" (Rom. 11:29). This is why you see, for instance, beautiful singers who God called to be worship leaders go into the world and begin to sing secular songs that don't give God the glory, yet they still have a beautiful voice. See, it's up to us to choose to use our gifts for God's glory.

Once you know your gifting, it might help you discover yourself in the Bible. When God gave me the gift of unsealing the books of Revelation, Daniel and 2 Esdras, He told me to prepare His people for the Kingdom Age. I began to look for "Benjamin" in the Bible and found "little Benjamin" in Psalm 68, which describes the transition of humanity to the Kingdom Age of the Saints. "Little Benjamin" leads the procession (Ps. 68:27). As I put together my humanitarian plan for the Kingdom Age, I recognized that all the people I met along the way and the experiences I went through (including the tough times), prepared me for the Kingdom Age – each encounter divinely orchestrated by God.

As we move into the Kingdom Age, the largest wealth transfer in human history occurs. For many, it will be like winning the lottery – a couple of years and sadly, these people will once again be broke. For some, an increase in wealth may even destroy them. However, others will allow the new resources to amplify their gifts and calling in a mighty way. Pay attention to how you treat people, stay humble. Ask the Lord to help you manage the resources. God gives us Kingdom Age commandments to guide us on our quest to fulfill the high calling.

Kingdom Age Commands

In *KAS*, I showed how a description of the Kingdom Age of the Saints is contained in a riddle in the book of Revelation. The "out of place" scriptures in Jesus' exhortation to the seven churches, when combined, constitute a detailed description of the Kingdom Age. It's a time of longevity, abundance, and victory. In Matthew 25, Jesus gives us a picture of the Kingdom Age when He shares the parable of the ten virgins and also the master who endows talents with his servants and expects His servants to make a return on the talents. In today's dollars, a talent of gold represents over two-million dollars in value! In Ezra's dream, God shows us further details on the Kingdom Age of the Saints and lays out a number of commandments for the age. The description begins:

> Thus says the Lord to Ezra: Tell my people that I will give them the kingdom of Jerusalem, which I was going to give to Israel. Moreover, I will take back to myself their glory, and will give to these others the everlasting habitations, which I had prepared for Israel. The tree of life shall give them fragrant perfume, and they shall neither toil nor become weary (2 Esdras 2:10-12 NRSV).

These verses speak of the glory of God which formerly rested in the Israelite Temple, being given to the people of God – in

222

our homes. Once again, God promises to fill the earth with His glory. Notice God again references the Tree of Life, as He did in Revelation 2:7. The Kingdom Age of the Saints returns man back to a type of the Garden of Eden. Here we neither toil nor become weary, both of which were part of the curse that came upon Adam and Eve in the Garden. It appears the curse is lifted in the Kingdom Age. The passage continues with commands:

> The kingdom is already prepared for you: watch. Take heaven and earth to witness; for I have broken the evil in pieces, and created the good: for I live, saith the Lord.
>
> Mother, embrace thy children, and bring them up with gladness, make their feet as fast as a pillar: for I have chosen thee, saith the Lord. And those that be dead will I raise up again from their places, and bring them out of the graves: for I have known my name in Israel. Fear not, thou mother of the children: for I have chosen thee, saith the Lord (vv. 13b-17 KJV).

Again, God states the Kingdom Age of the Saints is already prepared. We also get a picture of the Stone Judgment, for the Word says: "I have broken the evil in pieces." In the passage, we see a mysterious scripture about "those that be dead will I raise up again from their places, and bring them out of the graves." This scripture aligns with Daniel 12:2 (CEV) which states, "Many of those who lie dead in the ground will rise from death. Some of them will be given eternal life, and

others will receive nothing but eternal shame and disgrace."
The Lord has not yet given me full revelation on these verses.
It could mean a spiritual transformation – that saints arise
from our sleep and deception. It could also mean a physical
rising. In Revelation 6:11, the fifth seal, the Lord tells the
martyrs they should *wait* for the judgment of evil – are they
waiting for a type of resurrection? In the sixth seal,
synonymous with the Stone Judgment in Daniel 2, evil is
judged. Does this mean that some of these martyred saints
rise? I don't know for sure.

Note that mothers are exhorted in the passage above,
twice. As we continue reading, we will see *five additional
references* to children, for a total of *seven references*. I believe
this speaks to a major "baby boom." The fourth beast worked
overtime through abortion to murder over a billion babies in
the womb since 1920.[137] Moreover, the fourth beast actively
poisons our water, food and environment. Birthrates
worldwide are slowing and in some countries, shrinking. I
believe Satan knows his time is short and wants to rob
humanity of the Kingdom Age of the Saints. Perhaps certain
among the dead are destined for the Kingdom Age and God
raises them up.

If you recall, when God raised Jesus from the dead,
many graves opened. Matthew 27:52-53 says, "Graves opened,
and many of God's people were raised to life. They left their
graves, and after Jesus had risen to life, they went into the
holy city, where they were seen by many people." When Jesus
rose, a major judgment occurred in hell, when God judged

---

[137] W. Robert Johnston and Thomas Jacobsen, *Abortion Worldwide Report: 100 Nations, 1 Century, 1 Billion Babies,* (Colorado Springs, CO: GLC, 2017).

Satan and Jesus took the keys of death and hell (Rev 1:18). Could people rise from the graves during the Stone Judgment? Possibly.

Reboot of the World

During the Kingdom Age, God unlocks amazing gifts that transform society. After two thousand years, the often prayed Lord's prayer comes to pass: "Thy kingdom come, Thy will be done in earth, as *it is* in heaven" (Matt. 6:10 KJV). Continuing in 2 Esdras, we see how God reboots the earth with His Kingdom:

> For thy help will I send my servants Esay and Jeremy, after whose counsel I have sanctified and prepared for thee twelve trees laden with divers fruits, And as many fountains flowing with milk and honey, and seven mighty mountains, whereupon there grow roses and lilies, whereby I will fill thy children with joy (2 Esdras 2:18-19).

In the dream God gives His people twelve trees with varying fruit and twelve fountains flowing with milk and honey. The trees John also saw in Heaven in Revelation 22:2. The leaves of these trees are for the healing of the nations. The twelve fountains flowing with milk and honey, symbolizing physical nourishment related to milk as well as spiritual nourishment related to honey. In Ezekiel 3:3, eating a scroll containing God's Word tasted like honey for Ezekiel. I believe God blesses His saints with supernatural desire for His word so that their spirits are nourished and exceedingly strong. Milk and honey in the Bible symbolizes God's amazing outpouring of blessing. The fruit of the twelve trees serve to heal our nations of all remnants of the fourth beast, replacing beauty for ashes.

As the nations heal, we find out the seven mighty mountains representing the seven pillars of society, are now filled with roses and lilies – beautifully transformed. The seven mountains include religion, family, education, business, government, media, and arts. What is now riddled with ugliness and satanism becomes beautiful again! Note that these seven mountains now fill children with joy. Today, all seven mountains are designed to induce fear and anxiety, but that will change in the Kingdom Age.

Destiny of the Church

In *KAS*, I mention I believe God called the Church to take care of the needy. Instead, we relegated large portions of our duty to the government, who arguably did a terrible job. Government welfare represents bondage and servitude for many. God gives the Church another chance in the Kingdom Age and provides clear direction:

> Do right to the widow, judge for the fatherless, give to the poor, defend the orphan, clothe the naked, Heal the broken and the weak, laugh not a lame man to scorn, defend the maimed, and let the blind man come into the sight of my clearness. Keep the old and young within thy walls. Wheresoever thou findest the dead, take them and

bury them, and I will give thee the first place in my resurrection (2 Esdras 2:20-23 KJV).

God's commands in 2 Esdras 2 are consistent with His commands in Matthew 25. We are to do right with widows, orphans, the poor and the naked. We are to bring healing for the broken and weak. We are to eliminate scorn from our being and instead bear one anothers' burdens. (See also Gal. 6:2). We are to treasure the old and the young and give them shelter. Finally, if we see the unburied dead, we are to give them a proper burial. In other words, we are to be Christ-like. These wonderful commandments give us a framework for how we are to act and behave in the Kingdom Age of the Saints.

Rest, Protection and Restoration

The final commands for the Kingdom Age start with rest and quietness. Two Esdras 2:24 states, "Pause and be quiet, my people, because your rest will come" (NRSV). In Chapter 9, I mention the true rest from God still remains – it's in the Kingdom Age that saints experience rest. God prepares His children for the rest. So many people I know right now have businesses on hold and are being forced into a place of quietness. I believe this is God's doing to prepare us for the Kingdom Age. In this precious time, we must learn to recognize the voice of God as a dear friend.

As the dying fourth beast writhes in pain and agony prior to his death, he lashes out. However, God promises divine protection and peace as we hold onto Him tightly. God also provides additional amazing promises for the Kingdom Age:

> Good nurse, nourish your children; strengthen their feet. Not one of the servants whom I have given you will perish, for I will require them from among your number. Do not be anxious, for when the day of tribulation and anguish comes, others shall weep and be sorrowful, but you shall rejoice and have abundance. The nations shall envy you, but they shall not be able to do anything against you, says the Lord. My power will protect you, so that your children may not see hell (vv. 25-29).
>
> Rejoice, O mother, with your children, because I will deliver you, says the Lord. Remember your children that sleep, because I will bring them out of the hiding places of the earth, and will show mercy to them; for I am merciful, says the Lord Almighty. Embrace your children until I come, and proclaim mercy to them; because my springs run over, and my grace will not fail (vv. 30-32).

Tribulation and anguish precedes the Kingdom Age but God promises to protect us *and our children* during this time. We need to rest in His promise of protection! In the final passage, God gives a promise to mothers who lost children. I immediately think of babies aborted or poisoned to death with vaccines. God promises to "bring them out of the hiding places of the earth." Could this be the dead that rise? Oh, the joy if so! I lost a brother to disease and my oldest sister died at the age of four. Almost 80 years later, my mother still thinks about her. What if God redeems this time?

God planned a glorious future for us. He intends to conform us to the image of His Son and then allow us to dominate the world. He wants us to be a part of His plan. He wants us to heal the sick, cleanse the lepers, raise the dead and cast out demons. Freely we received, freely we should give. Jesus paid a heavy price for us to receive the gift of salvation. Our gift back to God includes fulfilling His destiny for us and acting on His commands.

Saints, God planned an age for us that exceeds anything we ever heard of. The Kingdom Age of the Saints represents a glorious time, a time of returning to the Garden of Eden and enjoying our earth, ruled by people possessing a pure heart. In the next chapter, I will cover ways to get ready for this glorious time. Rejoice and take heart, saints of God!

12. The Great Awakening

You gave the command, and a chorus of women told what had happened: "Kings and their armies retreated and ran, and everything they left is now being divided. And for those who stayed back to guard the sheep, there are metal doves with silver-coated wings and shiny gold feathers."

– Ps. 68:11-13 CEV

Society begins to wake up to the tyranny of the fourth beast in exponentially accelerating numbers. Can you feel it? Humanity begins to sense something good in store. A new joy and appreciation for life begins to take hold.

The fourth beast, now exposed, flails wildly while the tools of the tyranny-trade fail to work like they used to. The conference theme for the 2024 Davos World Economic Forum is "Rebuilding Trust."[138] The title alone tells us they know the public knows who they are. The enemy lost his cover, and now it's only a matter of time before his armor fails. The armor of the fourth beast includes the financial system, comprised of private-central-banks around the world that subvert the sovereignty of nations. For the first time in history, these same banks lose trillions and are insolvent.[139] The second part of the armor of the fourth beast includes complicit governments. Citizens worldwide protest the tyrannical actions of their corrupt governments. In Germany, thousands of farmers showed up to protest new taxes, bringing several cities to a standstill.[140] In Staten Island, New York, local residents showed up in force to reject the policies of Joe Biden that dump illegal immigrants in their communities.[141] The people begin to resist tyranny on a broad

[138]   Bicer, Aysu. "World Economic Forum 2024 kicks off in Davos with 'Rebuilding Trust' as key theme." *AA*, January 15, 2024. https://www.aa.com.tr/en/economy/world-economic-forum-2024-kicks-off-in-davos-with-rebuilding-trust-as-key-theme/3109157

[139]   Timiraos, Nick. "Fed Posts Largest-Ever Annual Operating Loss." *Wall Street Journal*, January 12, 2024. https://www.wsj.com/economy/central-banking/fed-posts-largest-ever-annual-operating-loss-6e249a39

[140]   Connolly, Kate. "Thousands of tractors block Berlin as farmers protest over fuel subsidy cuts." *The Guardian,* January 15, 2024. https://www.theguardian.com/world/2024/jan/15/thousands-tractors-block-berlin-farmers-protest-fuel-subsidy-cuts

[141]   Garsd, Jasmine. "On N.Y.'s Staten Island, anti-immigration protests intensify as migrants stream in." *NPR,* September 27, 2023.

scale. These actions are just the beginning of the Great Awakening.

In the Bible, it says the fourth beast dies slowly at first, then suddenly. Daniel 7:26 (AMPC) says, "But the judgment shall be set [by the court of the Most High], and they shall take away his dominion to consume it [gradually] and to destroy it [suddenly] in the end." Consider also Revelation 18:17 which states, "Because in one [single] hour all the vast wealth has been destroyed (wiped out). And all ship captains *and* pilots, navigators and all who live by seafaring, the crews and all who ply their trade on the sea, stood a long way off." Saints, the judgment of the fourth beast culminates in a *single hour!* Note the reference to seafaring. The maritime law system of the fourth beast collapses and Soldier Saints replace it with common law based on biblical principles. Also, the scripture mentions God wipes out the wealth of the fourth beast – where does it go? To God's people, the Soldier Saints.

Death Army

When God judged Pharaoh in ancient Egypt, a death angel executed the tenth and final judgment on Pharaoh and the people of Egypt. The death angel killed the firstborn throughout Egypt – both man and beast (see Exodus 12). After this, Pharaoh finally agreed to let God's people go.

The judgment of the fourth beast involves a host of death angels – possessing more power and authority than the single death angel in the time of Egypt. The slavery of the

https://www.npr.org/2023/09/27/1201878358/migrants-staten-island-anti-immigration-protests-newyork times of the Gentiles extended over humanity for nearly 3,000 years, encompassing all of the pagan empires of Babylon, Medo-Persia, Greece and Rome. God allowed the Rome-rooted fourth beast, the most vicious and cruel of all, to rule the earth for 2,150 years, five times longer than Pharaoh in Egypt. However, the warrior-host assembled for the task of judging the fourth beast represents a unique angelic army exhibiting unstoppable fire-power, assembled specifically to judge the fourth beast. We get a description of this host in the book of Joel:

> Blow the trumpet in Zion; sound the alarm on my holy mountain! Let all the inhabitants of the land tremble, for the day of the LORD is coming, it is near—a day of darkness and gloom, a day of clouds and thick darkness! Like blackness spread upon the mountains, a great and powerful army comes; their like has never been from of old, nor will be again after them in ages to come.
>
> Fire devours in front of them, and behind them a flame burns. Before them the land is like the garden of Eden, but after them a desolate wilderness, and nothing escapes them. They have the appearance of horses, and like war-horses they charge. As with the rumbling of chariots, they leap on the tops of the mountains, like the crackling of a flame of fire devouring the stubble, like a powerful army drawn up for battle. Before them peoples are in anguish; all faces grow pale. Like warriors they charge; like soldiers they scale

the wall. Each keeps to its own course; they do not swerve from their paths. They do not jostle one another; each keeps to its own track; they burst through the weapons and are not halted.

They leap upon the city; they run upon the walls; they climb up into the houses; they enter through the windows like a thief. The earth quakes before them; the heavens tremble. The sun and the moon are darkened, and the stars withdraw their shining. The LORD utters his voice at the head of his army; how vast is his host! Numberless are those who obey his command. Truly the day of the Lord is great, terrible indeed —who can endure it? (Joel 2:1-11 NRSV).

Note the signs surrounding the angelic host – the sun, moon and stars darkening – this mirrors the description of the sixth seal in Revelation 6:12-17. The host "leaps upon the tops of the mountains," symbolizing the removal of the powers controlling the seven mountains of cultural influence within society. Before the host is a land "like the Garden of Eden!" Once again, we see a reference to the wonderful Garden, where the Tree of Life grows. The Kingdom Age most certainly ushers in great longevity and restoration for Soldier Saints.

Many world leaders die once the death-host attacks – swift judgment rendered. In His mercy, God gave world leaders many opportunities to repent for tyranny over the past three years, and still a small window of opportunity for repentance remains. Every leader attached to the fourth beast system should immediately repent and ask God for mercy before turning themselves in to the alliance of Soldier Saints. Once this window of time closes, however, swift judgment follows.

When the death angel came to render judgment to Pharaoh, it passed over the children of Israel because they applied the blood of lambs to their doorposts. We need to apply the Blood of Jesus to our families, friends and possessions to stay safe in this time. God promised to protect us, but we need to be obedient. On my *Rumble* channel, I lead viewers through a short prayer on applying the Blood of Jesus – be sure to watch the video and repeat the prayer.[142]

All Systems Go!

Over-and-over in scripture, the prophets indicate that following the Stone Judgment, God's people move into the next age where the Kingdom infrastructure already exists and waits. I continue to meet Soldier Saints who beginning years ago felt compelled to build systems and architecture for the Kingdom Age. Author Scott Nelson wrote a book called *Economic Awakening*, where he outlined the new Kingdom economy, based on Levitical law.[143] In *KAS*, I mentioned blockchain-based infrastructure under development for many years by thousands of developers to facilitate seamless

---

[142]   "EMERGENCY ALERT: How to Prepare For What's Coming." rumble.com/c/revelationriddle. November 15, 2023. Video, https://rumble.com/v3vyqa1-emergency-alert-how-to-prepare-for-whats-coming.html.

[143]   Nelson, Scott. *The Economic Awakening: Using God's Economics to Change Your Family, Industry, Culture and World.* (Newport Beach: The Economic Awakening Association, 2023).

cross-border transactions with minimal charges, replacing the current banking system. I am aware of a group of ranchers that started ranching thirty years ago, because they were led to create the best beef (devoid of GMOs), and now they are just releasing their products. *Every* tool the enemy intended for evil, such as AI, God uses for good in the Kingdom Age. Author W.D. Wattles said in his book, *The Science of Getting Rich*:

> There is not the least doubt that He [God] will do away with plutocrats, trust magnates, captains of industry, and politicians as soon as they can be spared: but in the meantime, behold they are all very good. Remember that they are all helping to arrange the lines of transmission along which your riches will to come you, and be grateful to them all.[144]

When I read Wattles book, published *over 100 years ago*, I immediately thought of Pharaoh. Pharaoh pooled the largest stacks of gold and silver in human history on the backs of the gifts and efforts of God's chosen people. However, once Pharaoh fulfilled his purpose, God transferred the vast riches of Egypt to the people of Israel. Today's wealthiest families – controllers of the fourth beast – also assembled large asset pools on the back of the saints. As God did for Israel, He plans to do for His saints. If you feel in your heart that you struggle with a poverty mentality that might restrict your ability to receive the blessing of the Kingdom Age, I highly recommend

---

[144]   Wattles, W.D. *The Science of Getting Rich*. (Holyoke: Elizabeth Town, 1910). 69-70.

reading Wattle's book. His message greatly expands our ability to receive freely. God plans extreme abundance for humanity and we need to prepare our hearts.

Supernatural Awakening

The very angels of God are now involved in drawing people to God and preparing the way for the Kingdom Age. This explains why people are sensing great change in the spirit realm without knowing how to explain it. The Word explains:

> I saw another angel. This one was flying across the sky and had the eternal good news to announce to the people of every race, tribe, language, and nation on earth. The angel shouted, "Worship and honor God! The time has come for him to judge everyone. Kneel down before the one who created heaven and earth, the oceans, and every stream."
>
> A second angel followed and said, "The great city of Babylon has fallen! This is the city that made all nations drunk and immoral. Now God is angry, and Babylon has fallen" (Rev 14:6-8 CEV).

I hosted a guest recently in my home who travels America speaking to people and reporting what he sees on the ground. He said to me, "Something is different. The sky is different, the streets are getting rebuilt, new infrastructure getting installed. Everywhere I go, people want to talk about life and what's going on in the world. I've never seen anything like this." Angels of God are drawing people to God right now!

People are open to the Gospel. Soldier Saints, don't hesitate to share the Good News with them, that better days are ahead and we need to seek the Lord through His Son, Yeshua.

When does this happen? Jesus said He would rise on the third day, which could mean the Church, His Body, rises on the third day after being "asleep" for two days. In addition, God told Ezra the current age dies in 2,500 years, roughly 2,500 years ago! My heart tells me everything already started. I believe the Most High pronounced judgment of the fourth beast in the Court of Heaven some time ago and his death began. I mention in *KAS* the significance of the Russia-Ukraine war as potentially the final battle of the little horn, the controller of the fourth beast. Now Soldier Saints like Charlie Kirk and others are exposing false Israel. For the remainder of 2024, we will see explosive additional exposure of corrupt officials, pastors, and *anyone* involved with child trafficking or pedophilia. The exposure needs to happen. We need to *see* the organizations and individuals wrapped up with the fourth beast come to justice.

So how do Soldier Saints prepare their hearts for the coming Kingdom Age? What should we be doing right now to get ready? The answer may surprise you.

Immerse Yourself in the Word

Second Timothy 2:15 (KJV) says, "Study to shew thyself approved unto God, a workman that needeth not to be ashamed, rightly dividing the word of truth." Soldier Saints need to know God's Word. Spend time in God's written Word every day. We are blessed to have God's Word. The fourth beast tried to hide the Bible from humanity in the Dark Ages, but God made it available for us. Many Bible translators lost their lives to pay the price for us to be able to enjoy God's Word.

Every Believer mightily used of God needs to go through a period of deep immersion in the Word of God. For me, this happened in college, when I fell in love with the Lord. God blessed me with a supernatural desire for His Word. Digging deep in the Word of God began to change me – old habits died and my level of compassion grew for other people. To be clear, I did not initially possess a desire to study the Bible; Reading the Bible used to be my "go-to" method for getting to sleep! I prayed a simple prayer, "Lord, give me a desire for Your Word." He answered that prayer and I began to love reading the Bible. It became a treasure chest. I learned in the Bible that my Heavenly Father was better than any earthly father could hope to be. I began to call Him "Daddy."

Mark in your Bible. Use a highlighter or pen and scribble notes about what God speaks to you regarding certain passages. The Bible contains so many wonderful promises that we need to know by heart. If we read the Bible when things are calm, then the promises of God rise up in our hearts when the storm comes. Daily meditation on the Word of God prepares us for any storm. Listen to a prophecy by Amanda Grace on December 21, 2023:

> Start praying and fasting because appointed times
> are coming. Be sober-minded and vigilant in the
> middle of this. Do not let the enemy sway you by

every wind of doctrine or anything that goes on. We have to walk circumspectly before the Lord. We have to be in the Word every single day. We have to be spending time with the Lord. We have to allow our spirits and souls to be sharpened by the Bible to increase in wisdom in the middle of what we see happening right now.

The fourth beast begins to act like a cornered honey badger – lashing out in violence before he dies. Satan knows his time is short. The fourth beast truly possesses satanic greed. One who possesses satanic greed, when they recognize they won't win, then tries to destroy everything so that *nobody* wins. Satanic greed says, "If I can't have this, then nobody can have it." At one point, I did business with an evil man who operated in satanic greed. He operated as a suicide bomber. One can't reason with a suicide bomber – their zeal exceeds rational thought. The fourth beast tries to destroy humanity on the way out. Soldier Saints must find promises of God's protection within the Word of God and begin to thank God out loud for protecting them. Read Psalm 91 over your family each day.

As recommended in Chapter 11, discover yourself in the Bible. Ask God to show you where you are. Once you discover yourself in the Word of God, all fear and anxiety falls away and you move forward with a new boldness and zeal. You realize who you are and what God intended you to do on the earth. It might be as simple as being a great mom and raising your children up in the Lord. If that's the case, focus on that and shower your children with the Word of God every day. Knowing God's amazing plan for the future should give you hope and confidence to move forward.

Worship: Key to Victory

Hebrews 12:28-29 (NLT) contains a commandment for this time – to worship God. "Since we are receiving a Kingdom that is unshakable, let us be thankful and please God by worshiping him with holy fear and awe. For our God is a devouring fire." We must worship God every day. Put on a praise and worship CD or MP3. There are many worship compilations available on streaming services like *YouTube* at no charge. Start your days worshiping the Lord. Praise Him for the work He is doing in the world. Praise Him for the work He performs in your own life. Praise Him for tearing down the evil strongholds that are holding back His people. His anointing is so strong right now on people that worship Him. Lately, as I worship God, great joy comes over me. After worshiping God, new revelation in His Word begins to flow.

Revelation 14:7 says, "'Fear God,' he shouted. 'Give glory to him. For the time has come when he will sit as judge. Worship him who made the heavens, the earth, the sea, and all the springs of water.'" God created *everything*. Give Him the praise due Him. He sits now as judge over the evil fourth beast. In Chapter 7, I recount the actual dialog between Jesus and the fourth beast, as He repeated the words of His Father, the Most High. I believe this conversation already happened – the fourth beast was judged in the Court of Heaven. Praise the Lord for this. Thank Him for it. Then watch the whole atmosphere in your home change. Watch your estranged children come back to God. Watch all the fear and terror melt off of your life. Watch your appetite for fear-laced news wane. Watch addictions loosen their grip and fade away.

Heed the Prophets

The prophets are speaking at an increased frequency about the Stone Judgment and subsequent glory revival. After twenty years of tracking prophetic voices, I never saw anything like it. Each week I receive a prophetic update from *Flyover Conservatives*, a podcast run by David and Stacy Whited. They feature prophetic voices such as Barry Wunsch, Julie Green, Dutch and Tim Sheets, Robin Bullock, Amanda Grace and Kent Christmas. Other shows such as *Elijah Streams* feature Johnny Enlow, Hank Kunneman and Kat Kerr. These prophetic voices are a *gift* to us. Right now, ALL these voices are speaking of a coming judgment and time of freedom for God's people. They are not calling it the Stone Judgment yet, but soon they will as the Church understands God's biblical timeline more clearly.

Do not mock prophetic voices. Prophets are a gift to the Body of Christ. If you listen to their words, they offer encouragement and in some cases, exhortation. Listen to Amos 3:7, "Indeed, the Sovereign LORD never does anything until he reveals his plans to his servants the prophets." God always speaks to His prophets about the future. He has not changed. God spoke of the Stone Judgment and the Kingdom Age literally 2 to 3,000 years ago – forecasting a major prophetic event. The Stone Judgment is the next major biblical event for humanity. It should be no surprise that the frequency of prophetic words going out increases. Listen to the command in Psalm 105:15, "Do not touch my chosen people, and do not hurt my prophets." We can hurt people by disparaging them, or by judging them – stay away from this activity. If you don't understand a prophetic word, walk in enough humility to go to God about it privately.

God is raising up even more prophets to help us in this time. Soon, prophetic words of encouragement will be commonplace as the glory of God falls in the Kingdom Age. Learn to recognize and respect the anointing on people's lives – accept God's gift and receive from these vessels of God.

The Lord looked to this day with much anticipation. When Jesus spoke of Lazarus the beggar in Luke 16:19-31, I believe He was speaking about His Body. The ultra-elites of the world lived "splendidly clothed in purple and fine linen and who lived each day in luxury." The Body of Christ "lay there longing for scraps from the rich man's table, the dogs would come and lick his open sores." Lazarus means, "whom God helps." Only the Lord can help His people – enslaved, poor, wretched, abused, robbed, killed, blasphemed and scorned. For the last 2,000 years, God's people received zero justice. By faith, we are victorious. By faith, we possess our land. However, the whole world is against us and for centuries has killed, maimed and imprisoned God's people. This was the state of Lazarus. All but one of Jesus' disciples was violently martyred. These days are ending. The Word of God says they end and the modern prophets confirm it.

Stand up to Tyranny

Hopefully the powerful promises in this book stirred your spirit. By now you should know that, if you love Yeshua, you are on the winning side. God wins – evil loses. We are chosen as the generation that sees the Stone Judgment. God blesses the awake saints the most – the Soldier Saints. Begin to call out tyranny in your neighborhood, school, and place of work. Stand for good and not evil. It is resume´ time right now. God is looking to promote His people. He's testing us to see if we accept His call. The doors that open need to be walked through. Time is accelerating.

Recently I met with my friend Eric Metaxas. Eric wrote a book called, *Letter to the American Church.*[145] Eric shared he got more pushback from this book than any book he ever wrote! (And Eric wrote a lot of books). The Church eviscerated Eric for *Letter to the American Church*, because it called out the Church for doing little to resist tyranny. Most of the Church rolled over for the government-mandated Covid-19 restrictions. The organized church does not like it when people call it out. When I was with Eric, the Lord gave me a prophetic word for him. God promoted Eric to a new level in the spirit realm because of his obedience to God in writing the book. It took courage, and that is what God is looking for right now. I shared my own story about using my real name on *KAS*. It's difficult on our flesh to buck the trend; to be a fish swimming upstream. Did you know Soldier Saints that answer difficult calls will be the mighty ones in the Kingdom Age? We should no longer fear the fourth beast –

---

[145]   Metaxas, Eric. *Letter to the American Church*. Washington DC: Salem Books, 2022.

his days are numbered. Answer the call and watch what God will do.

Dream Again

Our best days are in front of us. We have the honor of living in the generation that sees the death of the fourth beast and the beginning on an entirely new age. It is the most exciting time to be alive! Let God begin to elevate your consciousness and see what He's doing – it's a marvelous work. In the Appendix, I share a partial list of scriptures concerning the Kingdom Age. It's only a partial list because I sense we are only scratching the surface of understanding concerning the Kingdom Age. A friend of mine felt led to write a book on the Stone Judgment, to be released soon. A relative plans to write a book on the Lazarus story as it relates to our times. Many others God calls to write new books and release new films. In 2024, more movies thematically based on God's Great Awakening are set to be released than any other year to-date – God called many to simultaneously release His Good News and also to wake people up with films.

As you plug into the Holy Spirit, you will feel called to do something. It could be to write a book, start a podcast or get involved in your community. You may also feel compelled to begin to pray for your neighbors or your city. The Great Awakening began – everyone has a part to play. Now is the time, Soldier Saints. Get your feet moving. God knows your name. His plan for you is in His Book of Life. Begin to discover that plan and operate in it. His *Blast of Fire* is coming.

Appendix

Don't Wait, Receive Jesus Today!

So you will be saved, if you honestly say, "Jesus is Lord," and if you believe with all your heart that God raised him from death. God will accept you and save you, if you truly believe this and tell it to others.
- Rom. 10:9-10 CEV

In this book, I talk about the judgment of God falling on the earth and the end of the current age. This judgment is not for God's people, but for the world and people that reject God. Now is an especially important time to know God and be close to Him. Don't wait, receive Jesus today!

God wants a relationship with you. Not only that, God has a plan and destiny for your life. To have a relationship with God, we must accept Jesus as our Savior and Lord. You see, sin separates us from God, and we must accept Jesus as Savior to allow His blood to wash away our sins and make our spirits white and pure. This is the first step on our adventure with God.

Receiving Jesus as Lord starts with a prayer that acknowledges our sin and asks Him to wash us clean as we accept His sacrifice on the cross for us. Nothing you have done in your past is too big for God's forgiveness. Jesus paid the ultimate price so that we would not have to. But we must, by faith, believe in our hearts and say out loud a prayer of Salvation. Ready? Say this:

"Dear Lord Jesus, I need you. Come into my life, wash me clean. Set me free from all bondage. Heal my body, mind and spirit. Wash me with your blood and protect me with your blood going forward. Fill me with your Holy Spirit. You are you my Lord and Savior. Give me the strength to serve you all my days."

Find a local church that believes in the miracles of God. Get a Bible and ask God to give you the Holy Spirit to show you how to read it. Tell others what happened to you. After your decision to serve the Lord, pressure may arise that causes you to doubt. Don't worry about this, it's normal. Satan tries to steal God's Word out of your heart. (See Mark 4). Stay close to God through prayer. Talk to God the same way you would talk to a close friend; you will soon recognize His voice. He loves you so much, and wants only the best for you.

Scripture References

Partial list of Scriptures Referencing the Stone Judgment and Kingdom Age of the Saints

Genesis 1:28	Habakkuk 2:14	Acts 3:21
Genesis 2:2-3	Obadiah 1:8-9	Romans 8:19-23
Exodus 19:10-11	Jeremiah 49:10	1 Corinthians 15:4
Exodus 31:17	2 Esdras 9:13	Ephesians 5:27
Numbers 14:21	2 Esdras 11, 12, 13	Hebrews 4:8-10
Psalm 68	2 Esdras 14:11-12	Hebrews 6:5
Psalm 105:15	2 Esdras 15:3-27	Hebrews 12:28-29
Isaiah 11:9	Matthew 12:39-40	2 Peter 3:8
Isaiah 34	Matthew 16:4	Revelation 2:7, 11, 17
Isaiah 40:3-5	Matthew 16:21	Revelation 2:26-28
Isaiah 61:2-11	Matthew 24:8	Revelation 3:5, 12, 21
Daniel 2:4-45	Matthew 24:44-50	Revelation 6:8-17
Daniel 7:9-12	Matthew 25	Revelation 10:6-7
Daniel 7:18, 22	Mark 9:31	Revelation 12:14
Daniel 7:26-27	Luke 3:5-6	Revelation 13:1-10
Daniel 12:1-3	Luke 16:19-31	Revelation 14:6-8
Daniel 12:7	Luke 20:40-41	Revelation 17:16-17
Daniel 12:10	Luke 24:7	Revelation 18
Hosea 6:1-3	Luke 13:32	Revelation 19:1-8
Joel 2:1-11	John 2:1-10	
Amos 3:7	John 11:1-45